# THE ENTREPRENEURIAL IMPERATIVE

"Modern industry has established the world market, for which the discovery of America paved the way. This market has given an immense development to commerce, to navigation, to communication by land. . . . The [capitalist epoch] has been the first to show what man's activity can bring about. It has accomplished wonders far surpassing Egyptian pyramids, Roman aqueducts and Gothic cathedrals . . . [and] given a cosmopolitan character to production and consumption in every country. . . .

"In place of the old local and national seclusion and self sufficiency, we have intercourse in every direction, universal interdependence of nations. And as in material, so also in intellectual production. The intellectual creations of individual nations become common property. . . .

"Subjection of nature's forces to man, machinery, application of chemistry to industry and agriculture, steam navigation, railways, electric telegraphs, clearing of whole continents for cultivation, canalization of rivers, whole populations conjured out of the ground—what earlier century had even a presentiment that such productive forces slumbered in the lap of social labor?"

—Karl Marx and Friedrich Engels,
*The Communist Manifesto* 8–12 (1848)


"The more people who own little businesses of their own, the safer our country will be, for the people who have a stake in their country and their community are its best citizens."

—John Hancock

# THE
# ENTREPRENEURIAL
# IMPERATIVE

★    ★    ★

## HOW AMERICA'S ECONOMIC MIRACLE
## WILL RESHAPE THE WORLD
## (AND CHANGE YOUR LIFE)

# Carl J. Schramm

**Collins**

*An Imprint of* HarperCollins*Publishers*

*To*

*Kate, Ellyn, Victoria*
*Three generations of grace*

HarperCollins books may be purchased for educational, business, or sales promotional use. For information, please write to: Special Markets Department, HarperCollins Publishers, 10 East 53rd Street, New York, NY 10022.

*Designed by Ellen Cipriano*

Library of Congress Cataloging-In-Publication Data has been applied for.

ISBN-10: 0-06-084163-X
ISBN-13: 978-0-06-084163-8

06  07  08  09  10  DIX/RRD  10  9  8  7  6  5  4

# CONTENTS

★

## ACKNOWLEDGMENTS

★

Benno Schmidt, chairman of Edison Schools and former president of Yale, once said to me that when a good professor brings a student to a new insight it is much like putting a ratchet wrench to the brain—once the wrench is turned one click, the student will never be able to see the world as he or she did before. The power of an insight that likely seems obvious is not to be denied.

When I became president of the Kauffman Foundation, I was immediately in the singular position of advancing thinking on entrepreneurship. Ours is the only foundation committed to expanding the role of entrepreneurship in the American economy and helping entrepreneurs along their path. No one in government was asked to play this role, and the handful of academics who taught entrepreneurship focused on mechanics—e.g., how to write a business plan. There really was no theory or research upon which public policy might rest. And the Kauffman Foundation was seen as the presumptive center of a wide social network of entrepreneurs, policy makers, academic researchers, and teachers.

My hunch was that Kauffman could make a much bigger difference in how the nation's future would unfold because entrepreneurship was not appreciated for being the subtext of American history and the contemporary economy.

Happily, I convinced Bob Litan, an eminent economist from the Brookings Institution, to come to the foundation. Bob joined a few inspired colleagues already in place. In no time, the collective thinking stimulated by Bob brought other colleagues into a wide discussion of the implications of economics and entrepreneurship. Contributing were an array of talents and backgrounds including Bob Strom (an economist), Lesa Mitchell (one of the world's most informed people on the transfer of intellectual property from universities to commercial settings), Rob Chernow (an entrepreneur who headed our entrepreneurial programming), and Judith Cone (who has enormous experience in the ways of influencing educators and who is one of our best critical thinkers). In time this informal seminar grew to include our general counsel, our public relations leadership, and an ever-expanding cadre of younger, brilliant researchers, including E. J. Reedy and Dane Stangler. Through Bob Litan and Bob Strom's seductions we developed a wide circle of renowned thinkers who became senior fellows to the foundation. This company includes, among others, Will Baumol, Paul Magelli, and Zoltan Acs, all of whom have contributed immensely to the conversation.

This now flourishing seminar had one totally unexpected implication for me. What I had hoped would emerge now would require a little leadership. Unlike universities and think tanks, our foundation is able to commission intellectual product. We can leverage our thinking because we can induce the best researchers, including research fellows at the National Bureau of Economic Research, to think along with us and expand the research frontier in entrepreneurship and policy. This research is, in our foundation's view, the basis of all effective intervention. To make sure that, when viewed cumulatively, all our work would add up to an important contribution, I found myself trying to create a synthetic view of what entrepreneurship meant to the nation's economy. In the end, foundation action should expand social welfare. At the very least it should do no harm. Just as in well-intentioned but ill-formed social programs, research and the theory it tends to support can be irrelevant or, worse, it can advance harmful policy recommendations. Sometimes economists get recommendations wrong—with disastrous results.

The first effort at a synthetic overview appeared two years ago as "Building Entrepreneurial Economies" in *Foreign Affairs*. The article sparked a great deal of interest. This book expands that inquiry and opens new terrain in terms of what we might be doing as a nation to improve our economic future. In every way this book is meant to act as a reader's touchstone for understanding the appropriate action to take when our economy is in such a state of dynamic reformation. It has been said that there is nothing more practical than a good theory. I hope this book confirms this view in a way that every reader finds valuable because of the practical perspectives it seeks to stimulate.

My thinking was greatly influenced by my colleagues mentioned above, to whom I am deeply indebted. In addition to them, my executive assistant, Linda Monroe, was supportive all along the way. These are but some of the web of marvelous associates, my friends at the Kauffman Foundation, who offer me the renewing challenge of writing as one dimension of management. The trustees of the Foundation deserve special mention for encouraging our unique approach of rigorous internal research as a condition precedent to funding our program activities. We believe this substantially increases the likelihood that our grants will have transformative implications. My editor, Paul Brown, taught me a new way to approach the task of making complicated material approachable for a general audience. To all, along with my family, who gives me much more than they ever receive in return, I am greatly thankful.

# 1

*

## THE ENTREPRENEURIAL IMPERATIVE

*America's future in the
global economy*

FOR THE UNITED STATES TO SURVIVE and continue its economic and political leadership in the world, we must see entrepreneurship as our central comparative advantage. Nothing else can give us the necessary leverage to remain an economic superpower. Nothing else will allow us to continue to enjoy our standard of living. We either support and nurture *increasingly* entrepreneurial activities in all aspects of our society and around the globe, or run the very real risk that we will become progressively irrelevant on the world stage and suffer economically at home.

In short, entrepreneurship in our businesses and universities; in our approach to both government and foreign policy; and in our personal lives is the only answer if we hope to continue to thrive.

Aren't there other solutions?

No.

Technology isn't the answer, since everyone now either has the same technology or can easily obtain it. By definition, when everyone has access to the same asset, the asset itself can't supply an edge.

Only innovative, entrepreneurial ways of employing that technology can provide a comparative advantage.

Education will not keep us out in front. Many parts of the world surpass the United States in teaching skills needed for the future. While we must pay more attention to education, especially in math and the sciences, simply drawing even with countries now leading, such as Japan and South Korea, will not be enough—we won't be ahead. We must learn new entrepreneurial ways to employ what we learn.

It is imperative that we do so: For example, we have largely given up when it comes to basic manufacturing because we simply can't compete globally on price. Instead of running these factories, we need to exploit the advanced skills, niche opportunities, and geographic advantages that will allow American manufacturers to succeed. In a word, when it comes to manufacturing, we must become entrepreneurial.

Could our financial skills keep us ahead? It is true we possess a substantial edge in finance. We have huge sums of money to invest, and our capital markets are, indeed, the envy of the world, attracting money to our shores thanks to their efficiency and safety. But the fact is that all capital markets are now global and other parts of the world are beginning to enjoy or adopt our safeguards, so whatever sustainable advantage we have is bound to be fleeting. The only way to gain an edge is to back entrepreneurs and share in their success.

The only uniquely American resource at our disposal is *entrepreneurial* capitalism, and it is imperative that we nurture it. We must make sure that developing entrepreneurial systems reward risk takers who set out to be creative and innovative, who produce a product or service that allows us to do something better, faster, cheaper.

It is the resulting efficiency of their efforts that permits wealth to be redeployed in ways that produce more wealth.

The message of this book is simple: entrepreneurship is America's comparative advantage, and we need to exploit it fully both at home and abroad. We have an entrepreneurial imperative. The pages ahead explain what this means and what we must do to achieve its promise. They also discuss the effect that the entrepreneurial imperative will have on our nation and on our individual lives.

Specifically, this book examines the four key components of our nation's economy—large corporations, government, universities, and start-up firms—and how different approaches to them will allow us to become even more entrepreneurial and what that means for us as individuals. These four institutions provide the greatest possibility for fostering entrepreneurial growth both here and abroad. Encouraging, managing, and supporting an entrepreneurial economy is central to our place in the world going forward. America enjoys both democracy and freedom, and this book shows that entrepreneurship is the force most likely to provide true freedom for individuals across the globe and here at home by giving everyone the opportunity to fulfill their potential.

Entrepreneurship is not only an integral part of our genius but also the only uniquely American resource at our disposal and we must exploit it fully.

## Digging Deeper

This book discusses what it means to see entrepreneurship as our central comparative advantage and its impact on the way we:

- Start companies
- Lead large, existing companies
- Run universities
- Make our personal job decisions (where and how we choose to work)
- Conduct foreign affairs

The starting point is to define what I mean by both entrepreneurship and being entrepreneurial, then talk about how the concepts can be applied in each of the preceding areas to provide us with the greatest comparative advantage and personal freedom and enjoyment.

> Entrepreneurship is the process in which one or more people undertake economic risk to create a new organization that will exploit a new technology or innovative process that generates value to others.

> The entrepreneur is one who undertakes personal economic risk to create a new organization that will exploit a new technology or innovative process that generates value to others.

As you can see from these definitions, entrepreneurship is an infinitely renewable resource. Every time an entrepreneur starts a business, convinced that she has spotted a niche in the marketplace or that it is the best way to control her economic fate, it is another step forward for democratic capitalism, a system of widespread participation and opportunity that protects political and economic liberties.

As renowned economist William Baumol has observed, the entrepreneur is "an indispensable component" of growth and prosperity—"the bold and imaginative deviator from established business patterns and practices, who constantly seeks the opportunity to introduce new products and new procedures, to invade new markets, and to create new organizational forms."

We must make such trailblazing occur more often so that America can maintain and strengthen its position in the world marketplace. Generating additional ways to help us become more entrepreneurial as a people and as a nation, however, will *not* involve institutionalized programs or new bureaucracies. Trying to make entrepreneurship formulaic is both impossible and a strategy that repeatedly has proven to fail. The Small Business Administration (SBA) is an excellent example of this within our government. To be blunt, very few entrepreneurial businesses owe their genesis to the SBA.

A government agency like the SBA cannot be effective in fostering innovation for two reasons. First, in the broadest sense, government was never intended to predict what entrepreneurial activities will succeed. Government employees, many of whom have never worked in the private sector let alone run a business, cannot be expected to distinguish good ideas from bad ones or offer valuable advice to an entrepreneur.

Second, in the SBA's case, the problem is compounded by political capture. The agency is constantly used to advance the ideas of small businesspeople who are well connected to politicians. The agency will serve the political interests of the White House of the day, and reality also dictates that this includes offering help to businesses they wish to reward.

If the agency wanted to make (low–interest) loans to *everyone* on the *same* terms, it might be effective in fostering the development of entrepreneurs. As it stands now, however, from the perspective of generating and supporting entrepreneurial ventures, it is not a wise use of resources.

But it is not just government that needs to change its structured approach to entrepreneurship. Businesses, especially large businesses, must embrace the creation of entrepreneurial cultures; universities must fundamentally change the way they operate to have more of an impact on the nation's economy. All of us need to become more entrepreneurial.

## The Impact on Corporations

If large corporations are to survive, they must become much more entrepreneurial—the key is to make strategy part of *every* corporate conversation, big and small. Focusing on where every idea under discussion fits within the overall corporate objective is the prerequisite for making the corporation more entrepreneurial—this keeps the company focused on what it is trying to accomplish and allows it to respond faster to changes in the competitive landscape.

Typically, corporate conversations are devoted to three areas: customer relations (marketing, sales, service), product and production, and the firm's finances. Making strategy the *fourth conversation* is essential. Moreover, part of this strategy discussion clearly requires a global component. Even a new technology-based firm in the middle of Alabama must contemplate the world as its market, not the state, region, or nation.

Start-up companies are particularly good at having all-encompassing strategy discussions, global and otherwise. This fourth conversation dominates discussion at all levels of such firms, because they realize that their survival depends on it. Bigger companies—where strategy discussions become more sporadic—need to model the approach of their smaller brethren if they are to become more entrepreneurial.

Accordingly, several key ideas will reshape large companies as we know them. First, bureaucracies will be radically streamlined. As companies move to closely align their organizational structures with their overall objectives, departments, functions, and people perceived as obstacles must be either repurposed or left behind.

Second, the trend of pushing authority down through the ranks to allow the organization to move faster must be accelerated, as companies realize that:

- Being entrepreneurial is their only true source of competitive advantage,
- It is imperative to execute strategy before the competition does, and
- The most effective way to make that happen is to give real authority to people who deal with customers every day.

Third, companies must actively try to hire people with the ability to operate on their own with a minimum of supervision. These people must incorporate strategy into every conversation so the organization will become continuously more focused and entrepreneurial.

## The Impact on All of Us

Every one of us will be forced to become more entrepreneurial. Without taking a stance on the current administration, that single sentence may explain what President Bush means when he talks about the "the ownership society." Each of us will have to take more control—we will each need to "own" more—of our working and personal lives. The ultimate responsibility of what happens to us will depend on us in a way that characterized the self-reliant men and women who settled the West.

The notion of the "ownership society" imposes new levels of responsibility on us personally and new levels of risk taking on the economy as a whole. Everyone is naked in the new world. No government can be rich enough or impose significant enough barriers—such as trade restrictions—to protect all of its people from economic insecurity. No institutional force such as unions can protect against the rigors of world competition.

We individually improve our chances of economic security by encouraging a world market in which hundreds of millions of people equip themselves with education—especially in math and the sciences—and respond to an increasing level of global competition in a way that best suits their own individual abilities to thrive in this new environment. This ability to anticipate and adapt to the future is what has always made America great.

Responding to challenges and taking individual responsibility lie at the core of our national character. Perhaps living on the frontier helped to shape these traits, but their origin may be further back: centuries of immigrants needed great faith in themselves to leave home for America.

While self-reliance partially defines Americans, we simultaneously believe in the importance of learning from our mistakes. This characteristic helps explain many parts of our democratic capitalist system, including bankruptcy laws that allow people to make a mistake and move forward.

## The Impact on Universities

Universities must make learning about entrepreneurship—a trait that is a central component of the American character—part of the educational experience of every student. Perhaps the best way is for universities to become entrepreneurial themselves. I would even suggest that universities should be encouraged to own and operate businesses, especially high-technology businesses, much like medical schools own hospitals. Becoming entrepreneurial in the truest sense—that is, risking their own time, money, and resources—will be critical to the creation of a risk-taking capacity within the university environment.

I'll go further: the market should decide whether a university itself stays in business. Universities should be permitted to fail and go out of business if they don't truly serve a need. The creation of new engineering schools and new "fusion" schools such as engineering and economics or engineering and environmental protection should be emerging, as they are at Arizona State.

## The Impact on American Foreign Policy

If we seek to spread democracy, our best interests lie with encouraging successful entrepreneurial economies to make the entire world wealthier.

Entrepreneurial capitalism produces expanding economies: as the pie grows, more people benefit from expanding wealth. More people own their own businesses and shares in growing businesses. More ownership will secure and strengthen democratic government. Expanding economies, as a rule, produce stable democracies, thus increasing the chance for peace.

When ideas, capital, commerce, and technology flow easily over borders, when we are increasingly linked together in reciprocal ways, and when times are good at home, people ask, Why risk what we have by going to war? If expressed as a mathematical formula, it would look like this:

entrepreneurial capitalism + widespread economic participation + stable democracies = a better chance of peace!

The inarguable conclusion is that entrepreneurial capitalism is our single most important export! If others copy our economy and if we assist them in doing so, we can expect our own wealth to grow. A network of democracies practicing American entrepreneurial capitalism will become a virtual common market more powerful than the European Union. The cluster of new democracies in Eastern Europe, if they settle on the U.S. model, will eventually force Old Europe toward new growth and stronger democracy. The apparent power of France and Germany to thwart American foreign policy will decline as other countries catch up to them economically.

## We Already Think This Way

This book attempts nothing less than a sweeping manifesto—one that will hopefully help change the way both government and corporations work and also the way we live our daily lives. In this sense the ideas advanced here may appear radical. When you dig into them, however, you will find that they naturally build on who we are as Americans and what we believe.

Entrepreneurship is a mindset. Indeed, some studies indicate that a large percentage of first-graders show all kinds of signs of creativity and innovation but that our school systems drill this out of students through a system of learning that presents a correct way—meaning only one way—to do and think about things. As a result, the natural impulse of children to be entrepreneurial is dampened.

The trick is to educate and encourage the largest number of people to feel comfortable with the notion that they can start a business, control their destiny, and contribute to society through their innovation and hard work. This is more common than you might think. At any given time, 15 percent of the population is running their own companies. Our goal should be to make starting a business as common as getting married or parenting.

Reaching that goal involves teaching the importance of entrepreneurship in our schools. As part of the curriculum, as early as high school, students should know that at some point in their lives starting a company is a very real option. And even if they don't start a firm, students should know that they will have a role to play in keeping big companies entrepreneurial and in helping government assume a role supportive of entrepreneurs.

On one level, it appears that to meet the future we need sweeping reform of how we live and work. But on another, it is simply a call for us to return to what made America successful in the first place.

This country was founded on the principle that a new economy must be formed, one in which only the efforts and responsibilities undertaken by individuals would determine their future. This freedom of self-determination spawned an extraordinary culture of work. This work ethic has always been part of America. Benjamin Franklin and Alexander Hamilton, for example, both expressed their belief in a national economy centered on appreciation, diffusion, and implementation of technology. To succeed in the coming age of industry through the exploitation of that technology, education—indeed, practical education in the sciences and "manual arts"—would be important to the new republic.

Every citizen would have the chance to be the next John Fitch, who developed the steamboat. Believing that hard work holds the key to controlling your destiny is a very successful way to live your life. The work ethic engendered by individual freedom and social mobility may be the most important reason behind America's economic evolution.

What is perhaps most interesting about the American work ethic is that it is most threatened when we become too comfortable. Our economic security is best served by economic discomfort. Whereas others might see the ultimate goal of a successful economy as insulating individuals from the insecurity that accompanies economic dynamism, it is this very insecurity that moves the economy at its core and enhances economic security. Yes, new companies and new technologies constantly displace the old, causing temporary hardships for those inside the established firms. But the net result is that our economy as a whole is stronger for it. (This theme will play itself out repeatedly in the pages ahead.)

One nation that outperforms the United States in any measure of entrepreneurship is Israel. When its just-retired chief scientist, Dr. Orna Berry, recently visited the Kauffman Foundation in Kansas City, I asked why her country is so entrepreneurial. She replied that Israel is, as a political and cultural matter, unavoidably insecure, and, in her words, the discomfort of this insecurity leads her nation to a life of innovation, creativity, and economic entrepreneurship as a means of controlling its destiny. Discomfort—and it may be intellectual discomfort—is the source of all entrepreneurial activity.

## Why You Should Keep Reading

Why this book? Why now? There are four key reasons.

First, as the numbers make clear, we are in danger of losing our leadership role in the world economy. We do have a lead, one that our entrepreneurial spirit and drive created over the last two hundred and thirty years. But others—especially in Asia—are catching up. We have all the assets and ability to stay ahead, but we need to employ them effectively.

Second, after struggling through a period of stagflation in the 1970s, we have reformed our economy through what I will refer to throughout as entrepreneurial capitalism. This force grows out of our entrepreneurial society and our rich history, our constitutional protections of individual freedom and private property, and our accumulated success in business. Being economically successful is in our genes, and we need to nurture and support this in order to continue to prosper. Our entrepreneurial spirit is the basis of our strength and wealth. And propagating our economic model will only make us stronger.

Third, it is critical for us to maintain economic leadership because it is the basis of our political leadership. And, whether we like it or not, we are *the* country that must carry democracy and freedom into the world. It is America's historic mission. President Kennedy said so in his inaugural address when he declared that we would "pay any price, bear any burden" to "assure the survival and the success of liberty" and that the United States would not shrink from "the role of defending freedom." That mission has not changed in the intervening four and a half decades.

Finally, entrepreneurship must be the basis of our foreign

policy—the American dream is not just for Americans anymore. Engendering economic success within countries is by far the most certain way to support the emergence of democracy. Fostering the means to create wealth in every country will make the world more stable. Schemes such as forgiving debtor nations have a very limited impact. Only when citizens can live in countries where wealth expands can democracy flourish. Failing to advance this model will inevitably result in a worldview that sees the issue of wealth through the lens of redistribution, not expansion.

Of course, the growth of worldwide capitalism will be good for us, since it will provide more markets for our goods, but it will benefit everyone. The opportunity to create wealth in an entrepreneurial way—that is, in a way that has it widely dispersed throughout a society—is the soundest approach to spreading democracy.

Developing and spreading entrepreneurial capitalism will revolutionize the world. It will bring stability, democracy, and expanded markets in which each country can exploit its comparative advantage. At home, creating wealth is the touchstone of our welfare and our freedoms. Every citizen should be prepared to participate.

Harold Evans and others have referred to the twentieth century as the American century. America can enjoy *another* American century, the twenty-first, built around the worldwide spread of democracy and the expansion of the underlying economy of democracy: entrepreneurial capitalism. But that can only happen if we see entrepreneurial capitalism as our chief comparative advantage and make it our chief export. Consider this book your guide to understanding how that can happen.

## 2

★

## THE ENTREPRENEURIAL AMERICAN

*Entrepreneurship as our
cultural history*

IN 1964, LUIGI BARZINI wrote *The Italians,* a complete (and sympathetic) profile of an entire nation. Hailed and widely read, the book remains a best-seller more than forty years later because the truths he captured about the Italian people then remain truths that help define the country today.

We are taught that generalized stereotypes signal hostile prejudices, but the reality is that one nation's people are distinct from another in such matters as culture, history, and religion. Americans are perhaps the most self-analyzing, and certainly the most analyzed, nation. We know we are different, and the world reminds us of that fact almost daily, in often disparaging terms filled simultaneously with envy and hate.

The perceptive American historian Henry Steele Commager spent a lifetime examining what he called the American character, and concluded that as a people we are enormously different from the rest of the world because we are all descended from immigrants. As a result, we are mindful of the perpetual newness of our nation and the extraordinary opportunity it held for our ancestors and continues to hold for each of us.

Frederick Jackson Turner, another American historian, suggested the most important feature of the American character was formed by the existence of the frontier. Unlike other nations, we had a physical horizon synonymous with a brighter tomorrow. We could always "go West" into a future that we could define and redefine as we went. It permitted Americans the chance to begin again if they failed somewhere else.

That was a huge advantage. It allowed our ancestors to take risks. If things worked out the way they hoped—if indeed they achieved the American dream—they could create the kind of world they wanted for their children and grandchildren. If they were really successful, they could give something back to the country. If not, they could just move on, knowing they would be welcome in the next place as newcomers who could add to the community and make it better. Their past would remain either unknown or ignored as irrelevant.

This attitude still characterizes all parts of America, and it is one of our greatest assets. It has washed over millions of Vietnamese, Guatemalans, Indians, Afghanis, and others who have become Americans in the last twenty-five years, just as the country welcomed all those who came before.

We are in every sense an exceptional nation and culture and were created to be exactly that. We began fully formed with beliefs that have remained remarkably consistent from the Declaration of Independence, the Constitution, and the Bill of Rights, through the Emancipation Proclamation and the declaration of war in 1917, which told the world that America would carry the burden for all as it attempted to defend and spread democracy.

Those beliefs continued to include the day we entered World

War II to protect and defend liberty; the recommitment of President Kennedy in the Cold War to "fight any foe" of freedom; and, speaking in Berlin, President Reagan's challenge to Soviet leaders to "tear down this wall," which led to the freeing of millions of souls living under the oppression of communism.

Richard John Neuhaus, author and commentator on democracy and religion, is correct when he says we are the first "creedal" nation. We have been a light to the world as the Mayflower Compact said we should be.

Part of our uniqueness stems from the fact that our founders spent a lot of time debating how the nation would be different not only politically but also economically. They were convinced—and rightly so as it turned out—that our new system of democratic governance needed to be accompanied by a new economic order. It is probably more than a coincidence that the United States proclaimed its "self-evident" truths and independence in the same year Adam Smith published his extremely influential book, *The Wealth of Nations.*

Ben Franklin and Alexander Hamilton believed that technology would differentiate our commercial life. They came to see that Smith was expounding more than a transformative argument in economics, that his notions about the importance of individual action, free trade, and the role of the state in managing the economy were useful in the context of nation building as well.

America presented a *tabula rasa*: our economy could be shaped in a way that reflected our democratic principles. The founders decided that individual initiative would be key in exploiting emerging technology. Hamilton encouraged invention, and Franklin, the consummate progenitor of so many American institutions, created the American Philosophical Society as a place where indigenous thinkers and scientists could discuss and refine their insights.

Franklin saw that discovery and innovation must be removed from aristocracy and democratized to create a new kind of economy and support the American political creed.

Our founding was thus a *joint* political and economic experiment that in time would provide the world a model of democratic capitalism.

## The Founding Fathers' Legacy Lives On

The influence of Hamilton and Franklin is felt daily. None of what we have achieved as a people or what we have given the world could have happened had we not been first and foremost a nation that could create wealth faster and with more predictability than any other place on earth. Our ability to build and maintain the world's most successful economy is directly and intimately connected to our individual freedom, our confidence and ambition, and our ability to take risks (knowing that if we fail, we can always try again). We are a nation of entrepreneurs! It is our birthright and treasure. Ultimately, it is more important to our future than any other single characteristic or asset.

As stated in Chapter 1, for the United States to survive and sustain its leadership role in the world both politically and economically, we must see entrepreneurship as our central comparative advantage. We must take that which we have perfected since our founding, our economy's entrepreneurial ecosystem, and push it for all its worth! If we don't, the U.S. will not only fall behind the rest of the world but also damage the vital link between economic growth and the preservation of individual freedom. We either nurture and support increasingly entrepreneurial activities in all aspects of American society—and help export this perspective around the globe—or run the very real risk of becoming progressively irrelevant on the world stage and suffering economically at home.

The good news is that the world increasingly looks to the U.S. economy for the keys to growth and expansion. While domestic critics worry—as they should within bounds—about our balance of payments and our current federal deficit, most foreign countries are studying (and copying) the U.S. economy more intently now than at any other time since 1945—and with good reason.

Even as a certain portion of the world takes joy in pointing out problems with the American economy and implies that America's salad days are behind her, the facts continue to intrude. Despite the post-Internet bubble bleeding of the equity markets, the mild recession of the early years of the new century, and the devastating costs that resulted from 9/11, our economy has continued to grow and, most astoundingly, has continuously achieved higher rates of productivity. Over the past four years, real gross domestic product (GDP) has increased by an average of 3 percent per year, while productivity growth averaged a robust 3.5 percent each year.

For all the ineptness of many corporate leaders, not to mention the recent villainy of others; for all the ham-handedness of congressional interference in attempting to manage and regulate the economy; for all the costs of corporate terror campaigns waged by plaintiffs' lawyers; for all the maneuvering of politicians who would sacrifice capitalism itself for their own ambitions for higher office; for all the rhetorical class warfare that is the ultimate refuge of populist politicians; for all the reliance on foreign investment to cover present consumption, our economy is remarkably strong. Indeed, our economy's ability to morph into new forms, to invent new institutions, and to support whole new concepts of how capitalism should work—whether it is the assembly line or the Internet—is probably its greatest strength.

The history of the last twenty years confirms a disquieting co-nundrum that is the subtext of this book: The *less* secure we are economically, the *more* secure we are economically. It is the entre-preneurs taking risks on many fronts and starting thousands of new businesses every day that makes ours a vibrant (entrepreneurial) economy.

Americans rank among the most prolific in the world at strik-ing out on their own and starting new businesses. The resulting in-novation is not a one-time event but a constant process. We improve, create, and invent all the time, establishing new companies to propagate the fruits. It is easier to establish a new corporation in the United States than in most other countries. In the space of a few hours—in fact, it can all be done while in your pajamas using the Internet—you can incorporate a new entity and have the all-important federal tax number for the new firm, allowing it to hire people and have its profits treated more favorably than individual earned income.

The costs of setting up a company are minimal and the benefits are both immediate and profound. A new firm may engage in law-ful transactions of all kinds. The individual running the company is for the most part immune from personal responsibility for the obli-gations of the new entity even if it should fail. This legal structure reflects our society's desire to encourage new business formation.

## Where We Are, Where We Need to Be

Our entrepreneurial economy rests on four institutions: (1) start-up entrepreneurial businesses; (2) large established firms that increas-ingly seek to operate in an entrepreneurial manner; (3) universities; and (4) to a far lesser extent, government. These institutions make

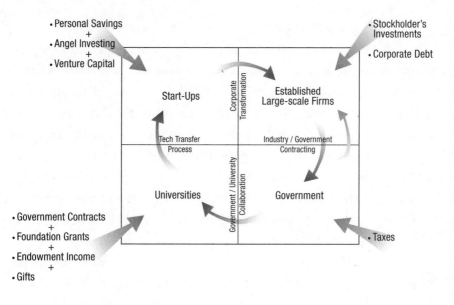

up our entrepreneurial ecosystem, and they have emerged to work together in a way that, from an economic perspective, might be called virtuous; that is, while each pursues its particular purpose, together they create an entrepreneurial society.

In fact, understanding the importance of the four institutions as being supportive of entrepreneurs and being more entrepreneurial themselves is growing. These twin objectives are slowly but surely becoming an implicit goal of American life.

This means a reshaping of society's values and norms such that each of us steadily and subtly feels the *entrepreneurial imperative*. Our society is making it easier to take risks and start businesses or to apply ourselves to transformative events inside the sector in which we work—to behave like entrepreneurs inside any setting in which we find ourselves. Of much greater importance, though, is the understanding of institutions, which often appears unconscious, of the role they play relative to each other in making our entrepreneurial economy succeed.

A nation of entrepreneurs has become an entrepreneurial society, and we reaffirm that fact in countless ways every day. Immigrants pour in and are absorbed by businesses, universities, and society in general. The business entrepreneur, vilified in previous generations (John D. Rockefeller most famously, but there were countless others), is a new hero in our society, exemplified by Google's Sergey Brin and Larry Page, Intuit's Scott Cook, and Apple's Steve Jobs.

All this underscores an overarching theme: while America is grounded in a core political creed, we unceasingly evolve and seek perfection, involved in something absent from the rhetoric and reality of other nations—a grand experiment. The entrepreneurial character of today's America is more than an interlude, more than a historical hiccup—it is the continuation of this experiment that will create our future.

The United States must export its approach to entrepreneurship. We have little choice because it is the only nonmilitary resource we have that can deeply influence world affairs and create a common purpose that will allow nations to exist in harmony. If we do not engage the world in our model of entrepreneurial capitalism, we may be temporarily isolated in our comfort but will quickly find ourselves disturbed by other forms of capitalism that are less protective and less supportive of individual freedom.

Before we export and expand our model, however, we must understand its true inner workings to strengthen and protect it against attacks and retrenchment. This is no small point, because, although not many people know it, American entrepreneurship almost disappeared completely not that long ago.

# 3

★

## OUR LAZARUS MOMENT:
## AN ENTREPRENEURIAL AMERICA REBORN

*The changing economy*

BY THE EARLY 1970s, it seemed that the dire forecast made by Joseph Schumpeter three decades earlier was about to come true. In 1942, the economist had published *Capitalism, Socialism and Democracy,* in which he predicted that capitalism would slowly wither through systematization, giving way to bureaucratic capitalism. The entrepreneurial spirit, the motor of capitalistic progress, would be stilled by process and routine. That, Schumpeter wrote, would eventually bog down capitalism to the point at which it would be replaced by a form of socialism.

And, indeed, by the 1970s, the American economy had morphed into the bureaucratic capitalism Schumpeter foresaw and appeared perilously close to a state-managed, socialistic economy. Economists such as John Kenneth Galbraith went so far as to proclaim the end of the free market—adding that it was a good thing. For example, in describing the current state of the economy in the early 1970s, Galbraith wrote:

The market itself is suspended by vertical integration where companies control all phases of the production process. In this situation, the planning unit takes over the source of supply or the outlet, and the transaction takes place within the firm itself. . . . If the state is effectively to manage demand, the public sector of the economy must be relatively large.

Our closest ally, the United Kingdom, was well down the path Galbraith prescribed. Its postwar economy was expressly committed to building a socialist state.

The United States, however, did not become socialist but instead experienced a remarkable U-turn toward a more robust and resilient form of entrepreneurial capitalism. This chapter briefly explains the rise of bureaucratic capitalism, then examines the factors that came together to not only prevent Schumpeter's prediction from becoming true but also to help us create an economy that today most of the free world is trying to emulate.

## The Rise and Fall of Bureaucratic Capitalism

In the 1950s and 1960s, bureaucratic capitalism reached its grandest hour; our entire economy could be described using the word *big:* big government, big bureaucratic companies that faced little competition, and big unions that limited wage competition and business flexibility. These three forces formed an iron triangle designed to provide steady growth, low inflation, and job security for all Americans.

The rise of bureaucratic capitalism resulted from a confluence of factors. Its appearance provides contemporary lessons for our approach to business and government, both in what not to do and as an illustration of how little developments can produce big transformations.

Toward the end of the nineteenth century and in the first decade of the twentieth, large factories and corporations began to appear in the United States: U.S. Steel, Standard Oil, General Electric, Nabisco, and many others, all exploiting the emergent nationwide market. At the same time, Progressive reformers reshaped government's role. The new concept? Technocratic regulation. Bureaucratic elites in public administration would manage an increasingly complex economy.

As secretary of commerce in the 1920s, Herbert Hoover pursued the model of the "associative state" in which administrative bureaucrats compiled comprehensive data and information and worked with business to further economic growth. While the New Deal extended this ethos through its wholesale introduction of additional regulations and administrative agencies, the federal government also began operating with a new philosophy that would reach its height in the 1960s and 1970s. The laissez-faire, freedom-of-contract capitalism that characterized the earlier era was transformed into a Keynesian mixed economy of public and private spending in which government would provide for the general social welfare.

In the private sector, technological developments such as the widespread introduction of the assembly line revamped manufacturing, helped the Allies win World War II, and, in the postwar period, gave rise to mass production in all areas of the economy.

This new application of technology produced innumerable cheap, high-quality consumer products. Economies of scale enabled mass standardization but by definition dampened innovation and creativity. If uniformity is the goal in order to produce the most goods at the lowest price, then the new and different are not valued.

The spread of mass production, standardization, and economies of scale mandated the creation of massive, hierarchical corporations, which in turn necessitated a new systems management approach, epitomized by the structures introduced by Alfred Sloan at what was then the world's largest corporation: General Motors. The result was the rise of the manager, William Whyte's "organization man." It is easy to see why some have dubbed the period from 1945 to 1975 as one of "managerial capitalism."

The Cold War led to huge growth in the federal government; growing union membership as labor tried to gain a growing share of the booming postwar American economy and massive defense spending; and the rise of what President Eisenhower called the military-industrial complex. All three factors were interrelated. It was during this time that the United States developed an implicit industrial policy favoring large corporations, tied to an enormous system of cost-plus contracting for defense technology.

By the 1960s, Keynesian economic policies had seemingly been validated: productivity growth averaged around 3 percent per year from 1960 to 1973, and real gross domestic product grew at an annual rate of over 4 percent during the same period—all this with low inflation. The result was that real income—that is, spending power after inflation is factored out—for a family of four rose more than 20 percent from 1947 to 1957 and another 13 percent from 1957 to 1967. In retrospect, this might have been *the* hubris moment for economists. Given this kind of growth, they believed they had perfected the Keynesian model for managing the economy, and most expected the economy to continue along this path.

With the economy "under control"—a situation the Keynesians thought would continue forever—believers in big government turned their attention elsewhere. As a nation, we took on poverty to share the abundance of the economy. In time, however, government antipoverty programs ballooned in cost and became bogged down by regulations. Escalating spending on the Vietnam War further drained government money as President Lyndon Johnson pursued guns *and* butter. As a result, inflation, which rose less than 2 percent per year from 1960 to 1965, more than tripled in the 1970s.

We were at the apotheosis of the New Deal vision. Government now saw one of its mandates as providing extensively for social welfare. The Great Society programs advocated by President Johnson produced a great bureaucracy and increased controls on business, spurred in part by what became known as the consumer and environmental movements, which added even more layers of stifling bureaucracy and regulation.

Had Schumpeter lived to see the bureaucratic capitalism of this time, he would have recognized the steady decline toward a form of socialism and easily spotted the seeds of deterioration that had already been sown. The Keynesian model was heading toward failure.

## Why Bureaucratic Capitalism Failed

Bureaucratic capitalism rested on the assumptions that economic growth should be predictable, government regulations should favor consolidation of economic activity in large corporations, employee welfare was best protected by unionism, and stable equilibrium was optimal. As a result, just as Schumpeter had foreseen, innovation and technological progress became systematized. Large corporations took over innovation and transformed it into a "science-based" process in places such as Bell Labs and Beecham Research Laboratories.

Foreclosing entrepreneurial activity was actually celebrated because small firms were viewed as inadequate. Galbraith, whose book, *The New Industrial State,* provided the intellectual basis for bureaucratic capitalism, declared:

> With the rise of the modern corporation, the emergence of the organization required by modern technology and planning and the divorce of the owner of the capital from control of the enterprise, the entrepreneur no longer exists as an individual person in the mature industrial enterprise. Everyday discourse . . . recognizes this change. It replaces the entrepreneur, as the directing force of the enterprise, with management.

Amusingly, a few years before Bill Gates started Microsoft, one economic textbook stated, "The era of the entrepreneur may be over in terms of the individual owner-manager who single-handedly built up a large firm."

As we can see, the slide toward a socialist outcome was not motivated by a Marxist ideology but implicitly driven by protecting the position of large firms (and their managers), big labor, and big government—the three elements that it was believed could keep the economy growing at a measured pace.

Ironically, the United States came to resemble the system with which it was purportedly "at war." Peter Drucker observed that, by the 1970s,

> In terms of political, intellectual, and religious freedom, the totalitarian countries (especially the Stalinist ones) and the democracies . . . were total antitheses. But in terms of the underlying theory of government, these systems differed more in degree than they did in kind. The democracies differed in how

to do things; they differed far less in respect to what things should be done. They all saw government as the master of society and the master of the economy.

Together, all these elements—large bureaucratic corporations, a massive federal government, reduced competition, systematized innovation, unions focused on the creation of formalistic work rules, etc.—carried the seeds of bureaucratic capitalism's ultimate failure.

The economy in the 1970s and 1980s started to crumble. Businesses, particularly in manufacturing, lost their ability to grow—industrial production fell in nearly half of the years between 1970 and 1983. The lingering costs of the Vietnam War, the growing costs of social programs, and the oil shocks all weighed down the economy. Medicare costs rose more than 20 percent per year in the late 1970s and early 1980s. Price inflation hit 11 percent in 1974, peaking at 13.5 percent in 1980, and the prime rate reached almost 19 percent in 1981.

The onset of stagflation brought sluggish growth rates: real GDP, after growing 3 percent a year from 1950 to 1973, fell to less than half that—1.4 percent annually starting in 1974 and continuing for nearly two decades. Productivity grew at only 1 percent a year, the unemployment rate climbed, and the balance of trade worsened. While all this was going on, foreign manufacturers invaded with fuel-efficient vehicles and contributed to the deindustrialization of the United States. The term "rust belt" suddenly was being used to describe the manufacturing heartland. The American century, it seemed, had come to a premature end.

Economists were baffled, and the apparent success of the Japanese economic model led to widespread calls for central planning in the United States. The cure for bureaucratic failure, therefore, was more bureaucracy. The *New York Times* in 1974 predicted that 1975 "could usher in a fundamental transformation of the American economy toward increased government planning and controls."

But bureaucratic capitalism, when overlaid with explosive government entitlements, could not provide the growth needed to lift the economy. It was clear by the late 1970s that it had failed. The only question was, Would we—as Schumpeter had predicted—indeed become socialist?

As we know, socialism did not come to pass in the United States. Instead, the American economy did an unexpected about-face, returning to its entrepreneurial roots. For the most part unintentionally—and certainly without any explicit policy commitment to do so—the American economy was reborn in the late 1980s and throughout the 1990s as vigorously entrepreneurial.

### The Evolution and Triumph of Entrepreneurial Capitalism

In a sense, what happened was the transformation of the economy from the iron triangle of big government, big labor, and big business to the virtuous box. The parts of the box are, of course, comprised of the four institutions of the entrepreneurial ecosystem presented in Chapter 2: entrepreneurial firms, traditional businesses, universities, and government.

Far from a planned development, the transformation and the subsequent dawning of entrepreneurial capitalism represented the intersection of myriad uncoordinated policy decisions. In every way, the turnaround can be viewed as a happy accident. There were at least a dozen factors that came together to cause the change. The reasons can be grouped into three categories.

First, certain government actions turned out to be absolutely

## From the Industrial Triangle
## to the Entrepreneurial Box

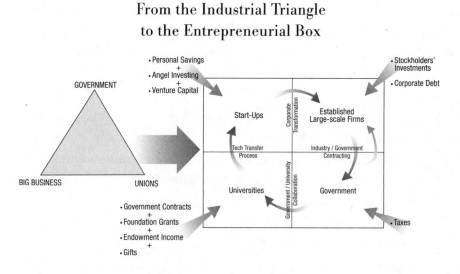

brilliant—accidentally. In 1971, for example, President Nixon decided to abrogate the Bretton Woods agreement that tied the dollar to the gold standard. Suddenly, the American economy felt changes in economic life in other parts of the world more rapidly and directly.

At first, the floating dollar contributed to the higher inflation and interest rates previously discussed. But one almost immediate result was to make the U.S. market more attractive to foreign manufacturers. As imports increased, Americans enjoyed cheaper and, frequently, better products.

Similarly, the financial capital released by the abrogation forced companies to streamline their operations and focus on innovation. When combined with the sudden wave of imports, however, many domestic manufacturers realized they would not be able to compete if forced to pay the wages demanded by big labor.

As a result, domestic production initially began shifting to nonunion states, primarily in the South, eventually moving offshore where wage rates were even lower. America's police car, the Ford Crown Victoria, was made only in two places—Canada and Mexico. Union membership, 23.8 percent of the labor force in 1977, was barely half that by 2004, and one part of the iron triangle was suddenly weakened.

Second, Congress enacted pension reform in 1974 with the Employee Retirement Income Security Act (ERISA). Employer contributions to pension plans increased dramatically thereafter, and in 1986, a modification to the law allowed pensions to vest after five years on the job. Employees thus gained greater control over their pension assets and labor mobility increased.

Importantly, a change in 1979 allowed pension fund managers to invest a limited amount of their portfolios in high-risk assets including venture capital. Not surprisingly, the amount of venture capital started to climb, making it easier for people wanting to start companies to get funding. In time, venture capital firms became a powerful force in creating and supporting entrepreneurs, because they funded start-up companies when banks would not.

Finally, the massive public goods investments of the 1950s and 1960s began to pay unimaginable dividends in the 1970s and 1980s. Worried both about the Cold War and falling behind in the space race, the United States had poured billions of dollars into university research in the 1950s and 1960s. In fact, in the 1960s, the federal government accounted for over 60 percent of all research and development expenditures.

The Airline Deregulation Act of 1978 opened access to discount airlines such as Southwest and led to a major restructuring of the industry. The result? Not only were more passengers traveling by air than ever before but also business travel became much less expensive, making it easier for companies to open new markets.

Similarly, deregulation of telecommunications and utilities in the 1980s saved consumers and businesses billions of dollars. Increased competition led to price competition and made it possible for new companies to enter the field, lowering costs further and spurring innovation.

In 1978, the Steiger Amendment (named for Bill Steiger, Republican congressman from Wisconsin) cut the capital gains tax from 49 percent to 28 percent (President Reagan further reduced it to 20 percent) and was a major help—in addition to the influx of venture capital previously mentioned—in making money readily available for companies looking to start and expand.

Government's decision under the Bayh-Dole Act in 1980 to renounce any property claim on discoveries emerging from federally funded university laboratories spurred university researchers to find commercial applications for new discoveries and innovations. University patents increased from fewer than two hundred fifty per year to more than sixteen hundred per year after the introduction of the act, and many credit Bayh-Dole with leading to the creation of entire new industries and thousands of new jobs. (I talk more about this in Chapter 6.)

## The Reemergence of the Private Sector

The creation of junk bond financing not only made capital available to small and risky ventures—companies such as Turner Broadcasting, MCI, and Viacom were beneficiaries—but also allowed "corporate raiders" to make veiled and often not-so-veiled threats about the need for entrenched management to start thinking about what was best for the shareholders (or risk a takeover fight).

For the first time since the wholesale introduction of antitrust laws, the power of big corporations was under attack. As a result, many large firms such as Disney were restructured and became more responsive to changes in the marketplace, benefitting shareholders. Moreover, the number of initial public offerings grew steadily, from fewer than one hundred in 1979 to more than seven hundred in 1987. These changes and innovations thus enabled Wall Street to supply more risk capital to entrepreneurial companies and to make existing firms more entrepreneurial.

Radical changes on Wall Street were reflected elsewhere in business. Declining transportation costs—as a result of containerization, a national system of pipelines, and expanded interstate trucking—connected the entire country to the rest of the world through imports and exports. FedEx, which introduced the overnight letter in 1981, increased the speed at which business could be done, as did the wholesale introduction of the fax machine.

The personal computer revolution, like so many technological revolutions before it, took a long time to emerge as a driver in American productivity, but when it hit, literally everything changed. It not only facilitated collaboration with people located in different offices but also spawned numerous other industries and innovations: software firms; infrastructure companies; new directions in finance and mathematics and statistics; and, in baseball, sabermetrics.

The structural transformation brought on by the personal computer—new methods of production, organization, supply—came into focus in the 1990s. A new type of employee, the "knowledge worker," became emblematic of the change.

The innovation of the Internet—the product of the Defense Department investing in leading-edge technology—is perhaps the signal event that made the American economy truly entrepreneurial. The Internet continuously exposes the nation to innovation and creativity, and allows new products and services to be developed at unprecedented rates.

Moreover, the Internet reduces search and learning costs, permitting larger numbers of Americans, as well as citizens of the world, to gain instant access to needed information as part of their creative process.

Intriguingly, the rise of mass-produced goods forced companies to start concentrating on the consumer. When goods are scarce, manufacturers can dictate what people will buy. As Henry Ford famously said about his Model T when customers were initially clamoring for the car, "Consumers could have any color they wanted, as long as it was black." But when there are more than enough goods to satisfy demand, consumers are in control. You could see customers starting to exercise that power in the 1980s.

IBM serves as a great example. With its near monopoly on computers, IBM was betting on another generation of large mainframe computers to keep it growing. But semiconductor technology had made personal computers a reality by 1980. IBM could not match the speed of entrepreneurs and younger companies that took advantage of the fact that it soon would be possible to put a computer on every desk.

The IBM saga underscores another transition that occurred in the economy in the 1980s. We watched the creation of business icons in people such as Bill Gates, Steve Jobs, and Fred Smith. Unlike previous periods in which great entrepreneurs were vilified as rapacious and un-American, today's technology entrepreneurs, often "geeky" scientist types, are appreciated for their sheer creative genius—and the money made as a result of it.

Certainly this was the case with the individuals who developed the personal computer and led the population into a new world where the ubiquitous tool became a part of nearly every American's work and personal life. Today, our children are encouraged to "be like Bill Gates." It has been a long time since parents suggested that their children should get a "safe, secure" job at, say, GM or Ford or with some government agency.

It was about this time—the late 1970s into the early 1980s—that we witnessed the dawning of a new public sensibility, one more individualistic than the collectivist orientation of bureaucratic capitalism. The shift was epitomized both in the property tax revolts in California and Massachusetts and in the election of Ronald Reagan, who appealed to individual self-interest as the key to general welfare.

It was also evident in the increasing number of entrepreneurial start-ups: firms such as Staples, Dell, and Home Depot were founded in the late 1970s and early 1980s. They were not isolated examples. The number of new business incorporations increased rapidly, from 319,000 in 1974 to more than 524,000 in 1979 and 635,000 in 1984. As early as 1985, Peter Drucker pointed to a "profound shift from a 'managerial' to an 'entrepreneurial' economy."

Finally, with the collapse of the Communist system, symbolized by the fall of the Berlin Wall in 1989, the world suddenly had to come to grips with the apparent triumph of market capitalism. Soon, former Soviet republics were expressly attempting to copy "American-style" capitalism through, for example, deregulation. (They had a model closer to home, of course. Britain, under Margaret Thatcher, had converted state-owned enterprises such as British Telecom and British Air into profitable private companies.)

But what these nations have been copying is a new kind of capitalism. While business and innovation in America have always been driven by entrepreneurship, today, ours is an *entrepreneurial economy*. In previous eras, technological innovations and entrepreneurship drove changes and progress in bursts. Now, primarily because of technological advancements, innovation is smoother and we enjoy extraordinarily high rates of entrepreneurship.

The information and communication technology revolution, though it had its genesis in the 1970s, has in the last several years produced a truly global infrastructure. Barriers have been so reduced that worldwide dialogue, collaboration, and synthesis—out of which spring innovation—can occur almost nonstop. It is now literally true that businesses can move at the speed of thought.

Another hallmark of the entrepreneurial economy is the constant creation and destruction of jobs and businesses. While tens of thousands of firms close every year and existing companies contract their operations and shed millions of jobs, an even greater number appear, creating millions of new jobs. The overall result is positive job growth and constant renewal.

Still, the upshot of a dynamic economy is the fact that it is characterized by increased risk. Many Americans now work in more creative and fulfilling occupations. The constant churning in the workplace has meant enhanced flexibility and more meaningful work for them. Paradoxically, the insecurity brought by this risk and flexibility has *increased* our economic security in many ways. As we have seen, all this new activity is what keeps our financial system strong. But it also makes our economy more Darwinian than ever. The cardinal rule is adapt or get left behind.

## Antibusiness Ethos

As compelling a story as is the rise of the American entrepreneurial economy, there are two thoughts to keep in mind:

1. It can be threatened and conceivably destroyed by express attempts to re-craft an industrial triangle of predictable equilibrium.
2. Seemingly innocuous actions—whether in business, policy, or law—can steadily accumulate and have far-reaching and damaging consequences.

That our economy can be threatened by a form of or a precursor to socialism is in many ways a difficult concept for Americans to appreciate, because it suggests a violent governmental overthrow. But, in fact, much of Western Europe has peacefully chosen a path in which social welfare entitlements, protective labor regulations, and high levels of regulation and oversight of business give the government enormous control over markets.

And, of course, as we saw earlier in the chapter, American politicians in the 1970s were veering dangerously close to advocating policies that resembled socialism. Despite the triumph of entrepreneurial capitalism in the United States, antibusiness and anticapitalist sensibilities remain strong. In part, these impulses spring from misunderstandings of the role of business in civil society. Many critics of corporations view business as somehow apart from or destructive of modern society. Others bemoan restructuring and downsizing as destroying a social compact that ensures job security, not understanding that the only way to retain our economic freedom is through a system in which the economy constantly evolves and responds both to market forces and our own innate entrepreneurialism.

Sometimes these criticisms derive from purposeful attempts to reinstate bureaucratic capitalism and import a European Union-style mixed economy, in which big business is "harmonized" by government. For example, Michael Lerner, president of the Jennifer Altman Foundation, complains that the economic "inequalities" and "pathologies" of American civil society—and by inequalities and pathologies he is talking about how our economy works—"distract citizens from thinking clearly about government initiatives that would ameliorate inequities, as so many European industrial societies have." This, of course, ignores that fact that unemployment in the European Union is consistently double what it is in the United States. People without jobs cannot think clearly about their role as productive citizens.

While many Americans implicitly understand that wealth generation is critical to civil society and human welfare, others remain ambivalent toward business in general. And a sizable part of the U.S. population, particularly the intelligentsia, sees centrally planned economies as the best approach, notwithstanding their indisputable record of failure. As scholar Michael Novak suggests, while socialism may be dead, anticapitalist sentiment is very much alive.

Despite the decided shift over the last two decades toward entrepreneurial capitalism, vigorous anticapitalist sentiments in the United States would have business comply with a wide array of non-business-related interests that could damage our economy and society. Many use the veiled language of corporate social responsibility to establish the presumption that business essentially operates in an antisocial way. Much of antiglobalism hangs on the assumption that business is always a malevolent actor. Such thinking purposely neglects the reality that only commercial activity can create wealth in the first place. A utopia without business has no wealth to redistribute.

The threat to entrepreneurial capitalism is perhaps best signified by the imposition of stifling bureaucracy and government regulations on business, and by actions taken and encouraged by government that attack and undermine business. Together, these represent the government's efforts to impose political goals on corporations, and each new politically motivated regulation presents real costs to the corporation that affect its ability to perform in the most efficient and effective manner. The call for state socialism could return if public and private policy is not consciously managed to protect and encourage innovative, entrepreneurial capitalism.

It is important to stop here to underscore the obvious. No sane person can argue that business must operate free of any responsibility to society or apart from government oversight. Government by the people is central to our freedom and success. And there is, in fact, an indisputable record of businesses rigging prices, polluting rivers, producing unsafe products, abusing employees, and deceiving investors.

Fairly enforced criminal sanctions should be used appropriately to keep business leadership conscious of its responsibility within the larger society. For those who lack a moral center, knowing they are going to jail if they do the wrong thing can be a great inducement to behave correctly.

But just as government must protect the public interest from predation, it must also allow businesses leeway and flexibility in fulfilling their role in civil society—which is to generate wealth for its citizens and ensure quality of life. It is my concern that the necessary balance, even in this era of entrepreneurial capitalism, is constantly threatened by efforts to expand government at the expense of the benefits of business.

## Bureaucracy, Regulations, and Lawsuits

It is a clear possibility that the United States can purposefully or inadvertently slide back into bureaucratic capitalism and toward a state-directed economy. One way this could happen is through the imposition of a surfeit of government regulations that hinder wealth creation or impose burdensome bureaucracy on business or both. While Joseph Schumpeter acknowledged that bureaucracy (in government and business) is an "inevitable complement" to economic growth and development, it can easily reach a point at which it disrupts business activity and causes executives to spend more of their time satisfying government bureaucrats instead of their customers.

Perhaps the best example is one supplied by Nobel Prize-winning economist Milton Friedman. He tracked the exponential growth in the size of the *Federal Register,* the compilation of all codified and proposed federal regulations. During the first half of the 1970s, the *Federal Register* metastasized from twenty thousand pages to sixty thousand. By the late 1970s, the total approached eighty thousand pages and, though it decreased markedly under Ronald Reagan, crept steadily higher in the 1990s and early 2000s.

Beyond the sheer volume of federal rules and regulations—not to mention those of state and local governments—there are various examples of specific attacks against businesses that threaten their operation. These include damaging lawsuits and the overreaction to the Enron and WorldCom scandals that produced the Sarbanes-Oxley legislation (see discussion below).

Lawsuits against business (including class actions), once an important tool to advance issues such as consumer safety, have morphed into general raids on corporations in the last thirty years. For example, from 1993 to 2002, the latest figure available (in large part because of the appeals process) the *average* class action recovery was $138.6 million. The average recovery of the top 20 percent was $613 million, and 2003 witnessed three of the six largest securities class action settlements in history.

Such attacks are frequently based on unrealistic standards of consumer expectations and establish a cultural premise that companies are out to intentionally endanger their customers, or defraud their shareholders. Additionally, the arguments and verdicts consistently ignore sound evidence that would exonerate the corporation.

Though there are unquestionably incidents in which business firms injure customers through intent or willful negligence and should be held accountable, the requisite narrative in each such class action requires business motives to be characterized in the worst possible terms, and, in many cases, the offending behavior is invented *ex post*. Think, for example, of the allegations against McDonald's for selling coffee that was too hot. A jury awarded $2.9 million in punitive damages based on the charge that the company consciously and deliberately made coffee so hot as to injure customers. Although the jury found McDonald's specifically guilty of "willful, reckless, malicious, or wanton conduct," cases such as this transform all variety of business decisions into potential bases for lawsuits. And often the logic strains credulity. Why would a company like McDonald's try to drive customers away by injuring them with coffee that was too hot?

Worse than questionable logic, these lawsuits implicitly rely on a cultural construct that says companies engage in nefarious schemes to harm the people—their customers—without whom they would cease to exist. As a result of this mindset, one of capitalism's engines—the quest for profits, which generates jobs and wealth—becomes suspect and the subject of class action suits. Many food activists and attorneys, for example, criticize the amount of revenue that companies spend on advertising, effectively indicting businesses for trying to persuade consumers to eat more, which is, after all, one of the ways they turn a profit. Still, this did not stop people in another case from suing McDonald's, claiming that the company's food caused them to become obese. Twice, a federal judge dismissed the claims. Still, these lawsuits greatly undermine any notion of personal responsibility by opening the door for people to blame others for their choices.

Class action abuses were partly addressed by the Class Action Fairness Act of 2005, which will shift more of these lawsuits toward the federal courts and may alleviate some problems. The legislation responded to many cases in which the certified class received only nominal rewards (say, a $50 rebate on a TV), while plaintiffs' counsel raked in millions of dollars. It is too soon to tell, however, what the real effects of the law will be.

Even if class action lawsuits are curtailed, individual actions against business corporations continue to pose a threat. The combination of a mindset that views business corporations as bearing blame for a range of societal ills and a cultural premise that seeks to punish corporations irrespective of countervailing evidence creates a highly damaging effect on the ability of business to contribute to and support civil society. Together with further government regulation and bureaucracy, they represent small steps toward bureaucratic capitalism.

## Sarbanes-Oxley and Its Consequences

Business is an inherently risky process, and is made even more so by the shift to the entrepreneurial economy. The response of the federal government to the corporate scandals of the early 2000s in the Sarbanes-Oxley Act of 2002, however, threatens to impose a culture of risk aversion on business corporations that could eventually endanger wealth creation.

The primary problem—and the one that serves as a gateway to other issues—is that Sarbanes-Oxley (SOX) represents a dramatic, intrusive step by the federal government into the way corporations are run. Traditionally, this has been almost exclusively a matter of state law—in particular, the Delaware courts are the lead actor since 60 percent of Fortune 500 companies are incorporated there.

Increasing federal encroachment means more laws and regulations, many of which are redundant, since they merely restate existing laws. The chief executives of Enron, Tyco, and WorldCom, for example, were prosecuted and convicted under laws already on the books. More pressing, however, SOX could have damaging effects on the business judgment rule, the traditional standard of review under which judges defer to the reasonableness of corporate directors and officers.* SOX institutes a strict liability standard regarding certification of financial reports by chief executive and chief financial officers. Rather than rely on the information provided by lawyers, accountants, and auditors, CEOs and CFOs now carry re-

---

* The business judgment rule "is premised on the notion that when a board of directors and senior management has acted with reasonable care and in good faith, its decisions will be regarded as 'business judgments,' and the directors and management will not be personally liable for damages even if a decision proves to be detrimental to the corporation. This holds true even if, in hindsight, these decisions proved to be unwise or inexpedient."

sponsibility for any "misleading" statements, even if they were the work of someone else.

The safeguarding of how the people in charge of corporations go about making decisions that they believe to be in the best interests of their shareholders is at the very heart of entrepreneurial capitalism, and the outcome of these new rules could be heightened risk aversion. Even one of the law's authors, Representative Michael Oxley of Ohio, has expressed concern that the legislation has made more corporations and their boards "extra cautious."

Indeed, more than heightening risk aversion among boards, SOX could potentially dissuade board service. The former chief justice of Delaware predicted that the scandals and Sarbanes-Oxley would "shrink the universe of qualified candidates who are willing to agree to stand for election as directors."

Bad judgment and misbehavior cannot be legislated out of existence. At some point, laws and regulations have only marginal, or zero, effect. As law professor Brett McDonnell wryly notes, "Ethics codes are nice, but of questionable importance. Ethical behavior is crucial; ethics codes, not so much. . . . Enron had a great code of ethics."

Further, one of the deficiencies with SOX is that its thesis seems to be that successful business firms (which help raise living standards) are founded exclusively upon processes and controls. Indisputably, these add to the integrity and proper functioning of organizations, and no economic or social system could long survive without checks on impropriety and illegality. Yet SOX erroneously presumes that bureaucracy is the font of superior performance. Laws that enforce accounting compliance will not prevent people from running their firms incompetently or behaving unethically, nor will they ensure good leadership. Visionary wealth-generating companies include, but are not built solely upon, good accounting practices.

Abuses will always plague our society and economic system, particularly during bursts of new technologies and attendant financial frenzies. This is part of the risk we assume in an entrepreneurial economy, and we must be prepared to deal with criminals without stamping out innovation.

Attempting to address every possible criminal violation can discourage innovation, and the costs can be extremely high. Audit fees of public companies have risen rapidly, averaging almost $9 billion annually, compared to $3.8 billion in 2001, before the Sarbanes-Oxley legislation. General Electric alone spent $33 million on SOX compliance in 2004. Companies such as Boeing, Caterpillar, and Motorola saw their audit fees rise more than 80 percent, once the legislation was passed.

But it is not just large corporations that are suffering as a result of the regulation. It also seems to be discouraging high-growth entrepreneurship through what some are calling the burdensome cost of compliance. According to a recent PricewaterhouseCoopers' study, approximately 30 percent of fast-growing private companies have either adopted Sarbanes-Oxley regulations or plan to. But with an annual price tag averaging $138,000, many small businesses are questioning whether the benefits of compliance are worth the costs.

Data from the Small Business Administration show that firms with fewer than twenty employees pay *45 percent more* in regulatory costs than firms with over 500 employees. More regulations serve to consolidate economic activity in the hands of large companies because they are better equipped to bear the extra costs. Ironically, then, the same politicians and government officials who extol the virtues of small businesses continually attempt to push us back into bureaucratic capitalism. Thus, SOX may help move us toward an implicit public policy that discourages entrepreneurs from taking their companies public and expanding them, decreasing the potential for wealth creation.

Concern over the costs and implications of SOX are not limited to American business firms. The number of foreign companies listing their shares on the New York Stock Exchange (NYSE) has dropped in response to the increased reporting requirements. While in the late 1990s the NYSE listed an annual average of fifty non-U.S. companies a year, in 2003 and 2004 that number dropped to twenty-five. Foreign capital markets benefit from those developments.

The takeaway message about all this: SOX is too much of a one-size-fits-all approach in an area that demands flexibility. More intense scrutiny at the federal level and tighter controls at all levels could have ripple effects in fostering risk aversion and undermining a key cog of entrepreneurial capitalism: risk.

Brett McDonnell, for example, observes that the "sheer number of new rules will force directors and officers to spend more time with lawyers over the next couple of years, and those lawyers will probably be giving quite conservative advice." This is a recipe for returning to bureaucratic capitalism. As Schumpeter presciently recognized, the "ever-present threat of prosecution for offenses which it is not always easy to distinguish from unoffending business practice may have effects on the conduct of business nobody intends to have," because it can act as a "drain on entrepreneurial and managerial energy," two engines of capitalism.

My argument certainly is not that government should never act to address shortcomings in the legal system. But, as in everything in life, there is a balance to be struck. It is my concern that SOX and its consequences may have tipped the balance too much toward regulation and stagnation.

Recall that one of our chief lessons from the rise and fall of bureaucratic capitalism and the dawn of entrepreneurial capitalism is that small, discrete events can steadily accumulate and, when aggregated, precipitate paradigmatic change. In this sense, it is not so much the specific provisions of SOX that are cause for worry but the *combination and interaction* with heightened federal regulatory enforcement, court decisions, and antibusiness sentiments that could presage a turning point for American capitalism.

## We Need to Remain Watchful

Thanks to the rise of entrepreneurial capitalism, we have overcome the restraints of bureaucratic capitalism and once again have a vibrant economy. Even so, we must remain vigilant. It seems the cultural default position is a presumption of evil intent among firms and corporations, so entrepreneurial capitalism is threatened. Though difficult to picture our system of capitalism as fragile, like an aging organism attacked too many times, its sustaining life force can, indeed, be endangered.

What might be done to establish an environment conducive to business and entrepreneurship? While policy steps are important, changes in cultural values are just as necessary. Simply put: We need to think differently about entrepreneurship. Specifically, we need to see how we can incorporate entrepreneurial traits inside *all* businesses, government, and universities.

---

*★ As the father of two children, I have spent a lot of time thinking about the best way to prepare them for the future. Here is what I tell other parents when they ask me what I think they should do to help their own kids. ★*

---

*Fellow Parents,*

I won't sugarcoat this. Getting your children ready for this new world will be hard. It will take more work than your parents had to put into getting you ready, because the risks are far greater.

Our kids—those now in kindergarten through twelfth grade—may be the first generation that could face lower standards of living than their parents. That can't happen in America, you say. And in the past, when there was no competition from overseas and government stood ready to supply extensive safety nets for everyone, you would have been absolutely correct.

But the raw truth is we are returning to a world where each of us will be responsible for our own success. Older parents and certainly most grandparents will remember a phrase not often used anymore. It was once said Americans were "rugged individualists," people who could take care of themselves, who were entirely responsible for their decisions.

Many of our nation's most famous entrepreneurs fit that description—people such as Thomas Edison, Henry Ford, and Howard Hughes. In modern America, we know more of these people. And there is a good reason for that: There are more of them than ever before. The number of entrepreneurs is not only much greater in absolute terms but also growing as a percent of the population.

These entrepreneurs, people who now create more than half the new jobs in America, are defining the new economy not just here but around the world. As you know, the days of the "organization man" who spent his career inside the belly of a huge corporation are over. Careers are more and more unpredictable, and the competition we face from around the globe is more intense.

Many foreign countries have distinct advantages. First, many have nothing that resembles our constitutional history that accords us enormous protections. In many emerging countries, there is little reverence for individual rights. There are few regulations. In essence, these countries can compete against us without the high cost of our legal and regulatory systems.

Second, they have learned the advantage that comes from investing in human capital. This is a fancy phrase that boils down to education. Because we have dominated science and business for over a hundred years and because the world speaks English (largely because it is the passport to our technological knowledge, the language of our graduate schools, and, accordingly, the language of the world market), the students of other countries have come to know us and our language very well.

The result: On any given Saturday in the spring, more kids in China will be taking their SAT tests *in English* than in the United States. Some of these kids aim at admission to our universities, to be sure. But many more will use their grades and test scores as their ticket to a fine Chinese university. And here is where it gets really scary. For every one American receiving a Ph.D. in engineering or the physical sciences each year, there are six Chinese students receiving their Ph.D.s from a very strong Chinese university.

Our international competitors have a third advantage, one we have given them. The majority of our children have lost what I call the immigrant's edge. Not all of our children, of course, but enough so that it is a real concern.

We still have immigrants who work very hard to be successful in America, setting the standard for hard work like many immigrants in the past. But while they still push their children to excel academically—understanding that education is the best way for their children to succeed in their adoptive home—many other parents have stopped pushing. And our schools, which once operated as meritocracies, no longer do. Today, we correctly celebrate and encourage ethnic diversity, but too often that comes at the cost of neglecting teaching core subjects such as English, math, and science.

What does all this mean for your children? At least this:

1. Knowing things that are important to the future is vital.
2. They will have to know how to skillfully work in teams.
3. The ability to communicate and process information quickly and thoroughly will be vital, as will the ability to respond to a rapidly changing global marketplace.

These are the three areas where you need to focus your attention and parenting skills. Let's take each factor individually.

Parents must make sure their children learn. It seems self-evident, but it no longer is. Our schools have steadily shifted away from teaching facts and the skills necessary to thinking and have substituted a values-based approach that spends an inordinate amount of time instilling children with a sense of social justice.

We should all passionately embrace social justice, but the job of schools is to teach children the basics of reading and writing and computation so that they are equipped to become economically independent. You don't achieve social justice by redistributing existing wealth but by making sure more wealth is created and distributing it more equitably by maintaining free and fair markets. And the only way that will happen is if children learn the skills they need to compete in the world today and have an appreciation of how the economy, when it grows, improves the welfare of all citizens.

The evidence of the failure of our schools to prepare our children with a useful curriculum is indisputable. The average American graduates from high school with a tremendous deficit in science and math. To cite just one example, American kids rank seventeenth in the world in math competency. In addition, they know very little American or world history, and very few have any competency in a foreign language.

In a world where schools appear incompetent to teach facts and skills, how can parents make sure their children leave home with the education they'll need to flourish in college? We can certainly lobby for better schools—and we should. But any change that occurs will come too late to help our kids. To offset the failure of our schools, you are going to have to create a new form of home schooling, one in which you work hard to supplement what is going on in the classroom.

The first practical place to start is with a shared understanding between you and the schools and your children's teachers of how your child learns. You must make sure that the school sees your child as unique, just as you do.

The typical school's default position is to teach with a one-size-fits-all approach. Insisting that your children are seen as individuals will take some doing. You will not be liked by your school system, and your children may be embarrassed by your level of insistent attention. That's fine. You are not doing this to be liked; you are doing this to ensure your children succeed.

Most schools pay lip service to the idea that each child responds differently to educational encounters (teaching). So the first rule is, know how your children learn. Do they grasp new concepts easily or is repetition required; do they learn better on their own or in groups?

Many schools periodically test students' aptitudes and talents. But they can be required by law to conduct more tests, if you believe there is a problem.

Know your rights. If the school administrators won't explain them to you in detail—and many won't want to be bothered—hire an education advocate (a relatively new specialty) or even a lawyer if you must.

Ideally, you want the school to give your children the same approach to education that it gives those placed in the "gifted and talented" program. (The content need not be identical; the approach must be.) Children chosen for the gifted and talented (G&T) program get a much different curriculum. These programs are geared to getting kids into good colleges, and that requires them to do well on standardized tests such as the ACTs and SATs.

To do well on these tests, children must know facts (e.g., the Declaration of Independence was signed in 1776, but the Constitution was not ratified until 1789; the Bill of Rights is not in the Constitution, but comprises the first ten amendments, as well as skills such as computation and grammar; that is, they must know things). The ACT and the SAT do not ask a child to describe what social justice means.

The G&T curriculum in many schools resembles the curriculum you and I had in school. It prepared kids for success. It provided them with the essentials of what high school children should know. Admission to the gifted and talented curriculum, or the creation of an individualized program for your children that provides something like it, should be your goal.

Many school districts say admission to the G&T program is based solely on objective measures (tests), but, in truth, many children are admitted in response to parental pressure. (Many more children of teachers are in these programs than you might expect, assuming intelligence is evenly distributed.)

The moral: In a world that will highly value those comfortable with math and science, you must make sure your children have an inventory of facts and skills and can use this knowledge to be creative.

Children must receive exposure to and master two other subjects. Geography is the predictor of so much in the future relation of countries, how markets behave, and what role various nations will play in the future. Yet it has all but disappeared from schools. Every child must understand the importance of the world to America's future.

History is another area of study that has been greatly compromised in our schools. While it is still part of the curriculum, the capacity of schools to teach history analytically has been greatly diminished. It is now often taught as a critique of western civilization where the "right" answer is that the progress of humankind in the sciences, business, and the arts must always be questioned. History for school children should be focused on teaching facts, and those facts should include how civilization progresses (which in turn should lead to an exploration of the contributions America has made).

One good measure of what your children should know is provided in the series by E. D. Hirsch, which describes the things each grade should accomplish. These books, one per grade, provide a very detailed benchmark for what should be covered. If your children are not learning these sorts of things in school, you need to see that they are learning them at home.

In addition, parents should provide encouragement for children to broaden their normal scope of thinking by visiting museums and taking summer jobs, once they are old enough, with technology companies. In the United Kingdom, every high school senior now spends five days in a technology company observing how a business really operates.

One final thought on your role: At home, the drive to set career paths in perspective is central. The message must be: stay in school and excel in school—at the expense of social activity if necessary. Also, make sure that your children's friends have parents who also expect achievement from their children.

What an individual knows is his or her personal asset. But individuals in the world ahead must know how to work in groups or teams to create valuable products together. One of the great recent commercial transformations has been the recognition of the necessity of teamwork in creating highly technical products. There is a reason that many of our most important tools of modern life—the computer, cell phone, DVD—do not have one name attached to them as the inventor. They were all fathered by teams.

To be an effective team member requires not only following but also learning to lead. Entrepreneurs are usually effective leaders, but because they cannot do everything themselves, they must also learn to be effective team members. Show your children what entrepreneurs and teams do. One fun way is to have them visit www.hotshotbusiness.com, a Web site jointly operated by Disney and the Kauffman Foundation that simulates the creation of new business through an interactive software program. Junior Achievement (www.ja.org) and the National Institute for Teaching Entrepreneurship (www.nfte.com) also expose students to hands-on education that combines team experiences.

The final piece of the preparation puzzle is making sure your children are ready to compete in the global marketplace. American business is now global, so everyone joining the workforce in coming years will need to be comfortable in this new environment.

Unfortunately, this is another place our schools have let us down. We spend virtually no time teaching about the economies of other countries, and foreign languages have never played a significant role in American education. That must change. European countries, especially the trading countries of England, Scandinavia, and the Netherlands, have always taught their children the languages of the markets where they wanted to sell their goods or invest their money.

Many people discount the need to teach American children foreign languages because they believe the entire world will be speaking English. At one level, this is true. In a matter of time, the number of Chinese competent in English will be greater than the number of Americans who are. But there is no substitute for a thorough understanding of the cultures and languages of those parts of the world where opportunity will arise.

Let me end where I began: you have a tough task ahead of you. Any parental attempt to tell children they should be prepared for a world where being a rugged individualist will pay off flies in the face of constant messages and images provided by movies and television. These messages say there are far more important things for your kids to think about—sex, drugs, and rock and roll, to name three.

Countering the media is daunting. Still, we must try. Every child should know that there are three rules for minimum economic success (i.e., not being poor): Graduate from high school, don't have a baby out of wedlock, and don't get married as a teenager. Everything starts there. For children who aspire to be more than "not poor," the most predictable path is to graduate from college (better colleges yield higher rates of economic success) and to delay having a family until a strong foundation for financial and relationship stability is in place.

Parenting is a big job in any circumstance. As we define the job as getting your children ready for life in a very competitive world where they will confront Chinese, Indian, Japanese, and Russian competitors, it is much more difficult and challenging. But preparing them for the future is one of the most important things we can do. I wish you luck.

# 4

★

## THE ENTREPRENEUR

*Everyone's burden in the economy*

AS WE HAVE SEEN, our entrepreneurial economy rests on four institutions: (1) start-up entrepreneurial businesses; (2) large established firms that increasingly seek to operate in an entrepreneurial manner; (3) universities; and (4) to a far lesser extent, government. In subsequent chapters, we will deal with large corporations and universities in depth, and the role of government in the ecosystem will be discussed throughout. This chapter concentrates on the people who start new businesses.

The start-up firm, the home base of the entrepreneur, is the single most important unit of economic activity in our system. What sets the United States apart is how many people view striking out on their own as a viable option. Each year, tens of millions of Americans are involved in starting their own companies, running their own businesses, or playing a lead role in a newly created business.

This reality is astoundingly underappreciated for its importance to our economic growth and diversity. We have thousands of experts on large firms: every year hundreds of new books are written by management gurus and business school professors, all designed to help those who run large firms do their jobs more effectively. Yet the critically important entrepreneurial firm remains very much a mystery. Experts on small firms are few and far between, and there is not much to read that is useful about how these firms come into being and grow.

We know a great deal about companies such as Microsoft, Dell, FedEx, and Intel that have become giant firms. This is because at some point they became huge employers, publicly owned, and competitive threats to other big firms. But what we know about smaller firms remains scant—the people who create these companies are almost a mystery. The entrepreneur is relatively invisible to economists and policy makers.

Why are these start-up firms so important? There are two key reasons. Start-ups are the engine of our nation's economic growth, especially its expanding job base. For the United States to continue to provide full employment, even in the face of what many people believe to be the problem of offshoring, and to accommodate the growing numbers of immigrants vital to our continued economic growth, creating new firms is critical.

In addition to job creation, the rest of our entrepreneurial ecosystem depends on these firms because of the critical role they increasingly play in the lives of established firms. Throughout our history, much of the technological foundation of our economy has had its start in small firms. These firms can exist solely to exploit a new technology. With the continued growth of the importance of technology to the economy, entrepreneurial firms have proven to be the most successful laboratory to test the commercial viability of an idea and to see the new technology through various mutations to the market.

The advantages of smaller firms in these kinds of situations are obvious. They can be extremely focused; they can be much more sensitive to market needs and demands (i.e., they can change course quickly); and they often have an advantage in bringing in venture capital to finance their growth. Our economy is dynamic because of the passion of entrepreneurial start-up firms and their constant testing of new ideas.

But what is it that ultimately drives more and more individuals to act as entrepreneurs? The secret is to understand what used to be called the "economic man." People always seek to improve their economic situation. Steven Landsburg has put it succinctly in his book *The Armchair Economist*, "People respond to incentives, all the rest is commentary."

Economics concerns itself with only two types of incentives: (1) positive incentives that induce people to behave in ways that are good for them specifically and for society in general, and (2) negative incentives (also known as disincentives) that keep people from doing things detrimental to their own and the general welfare. Not surprisingly then, the people who operate within the ecosystem as entrepreneurs are responding to signals that the market (or society, acting through the market in which it signals its needs) sends.

Perhaps the most important question is, what are the incentives and disincentives that produce more or fewer entrepreneurs? Understanding what it is that entrepreneurs see by way of motivation will help us understand who they are and improve the way our entrepreneurial ecosystem functions. And the best place to begin is with a discussion of risk.

Given our definition of an entrepreneur as *someone who undertakes personal economic risk to create a new organization that will exploit a new technology or innovative processes that will generate value to others,* it is obvious that there is no way an entrepreneur can avoid risk. It is inherent in the process of starting companies.

At the beginning, the risk of failure overwhelms all else. The embryo entrepreneur asks himself or herself again and again:

- Can I afford to take this risk?
- What will happen if I fail?
- What will I lose?

Indeed, these inquiries into the implications of risk taking are so integral to what entrepreneurs are that they really define the essence of what it means to be an entrepreneur.

The risk involved is mostly economic: Will I lose my savings? Can I find a job if I fail? What will be the burden I ask my loved ones to share? Will we have to drive around in old cars and live in too small a house with too big a mortgage while I pursue what might be a nutty idea?

But sometimes those financial concerns make up only part of a risk seen as something even larger. If the start-up involves leaving what others view as an especially good position, the risk of failure can be seen as a reflection on the entrepreneur's intelligence and judgment. I have known people working as investment bankers, in situations in which they could become very rich (with relatively low risk), who decided that they wanted to start their own business. Surely, they knew that if they failed, it might be impossible to reenter a job similar to their former position—Wall Street judges individuals harder than any other sector of society.

A story of just such an entrepreneur, Lindsay Held, was reported in the *New York Times*. Leaving his job as a corporate lawyer and investment banker, he started a chain of ice cream stores on the Upper East Side of Manhattan. " 'There's always the questions of the prestige factor, which entered my head,' Held said. 'But I said: You know what? I want to have my own business. *I want to build something.*' " (emphasis added). As we said, if he fails, having spent time in what has to look to his former colleagues as a trivial pursuit, it is unlikely he will be invited back into his former business.

Other people know that if they fail, they put their family at risk. I know an entrepreneur who has struggled to hold his family together while the federal government endlessly deliberates about whether his idea of selling a regulated product on the Internet is legal.

In yet another case, a professor at one of the most prestigious engineering schools in the country nearly lost his wife while he pursued an invention that looked for all its brilliance to have no market. His wife argued that his research career was suffering while he pursued his dream and he would never be tenured. (Thank goodness, at the last minute, the Department of Defense decided that what he had devised, nanotechnology involving a set of micro-scopic sensors and transmitters, could play a key role in the war on terror and gave him substantial funding.)

In thinking about risk, many entrepreneurs see only the upside. This is often the case, because—as is said of successful immigrants who start successful businesses—they have nothing to lose.

I am good friends with a Greek immigrant in Milwaukee, who, after a fight with his father over control of the family newsstand, scraped his savings together and bought a one-way ticket to Chicago. Upon arriving at O'Hare with less than $100 and speaking no English, Peter looked in the phone book for Greek-surnamed individuals. The second Greek he spoke with told him to wait at the airport and he'd pick him up. In a few days, he was washing dishes in a Greek restaurant in downtown Chicago.

Peter saved almost all the money he made and used this grub stake to strike out on his own. Twenty-five years later, he owns the largest cab company in the city, has substantial commercial real estate holdings, and his four children have graduated from college.

Millions of similar stories fill our nation. Every American family, it seems, can tell the story of an ancestor who arrived with nothing, took a job that no one else wanted—ragman, ditch digger, bricklayer—and eventually it led to a successful business and the ability of the family to improve their fortune.

## A Bit of Perspective

When we say our ancestors started from nothing, that is not completely true. While they had few economic assets, they possessed skills, knowledge, family, and their network of friends and acquaintances.

This network proved critical. Often made up of people from the same country, they were fellow immigrants willing to help one another—picture my friend Peter randomly picking out Greek-surnamed people from the phone book. They knew that a network counted long before business professors and sociologists gave it a name.

They also valued a great intangible asset: they knew America gave everyone freedom and opportunity. As a result, these people saw risk differently; the real risk was not to try.

None of this is materially different today, not for immigrants or for native-born citizens. While many pundits and professors see one problem after another, the tough-minded lens of economic analysis—and simply our daily experience—tells a different story. Visit the rural reaches of Kentucky or downtown Kenosha. You know what you will find: a family born halfway around the world who now owns a gas station, a dry-cleaning store, a convenience store, or a restaurant.

The data say it is obvious that the continuous stream of new immigrants reveals an "expressed preference" for life in America. Despite the skeptics who claim we are making the American promise unachievable for the poor and for immigrants, the opportunity to make an economic life that is better than what was left behind is palpable.

Just as in generations past, America offers the concrete hope that life can be better for you—and certainly for your children. The large number of children who are the first generation of their families to go to college, who attend Stanford, the University of Wisconsin, UCLA, and Yale, makes the point in a way that cannot be more obvious.

Today in America it is in many ways less risky to start a business than in times past. The most important factor that reduces risk is a robust economy. Since World War II, unemployment has been remarkably low, averaging less than 6 percent a year since 1959. Even in our worst Cold War recession, unemployment never exceeded 9.7 percent (in 1982.) This remarkable fact provides an important assurance to people contemplating taking the risk of working for themselves: if all goes wrong, the job market is most likely to absorb a failed entrepreneur.

Further, during the last sixty years we have built a fairly comprehensive safety net that provides social insurance for unemployment. While it is not much, many failed entrepreneurs have been helped in the transition to a new job by this coverage.

Finally, the nation's bankruptcy laws give individuals the ability to walk away from the liabilities their businesses incurred. Insulating the individual from the debts of his business is very important. While some would argue that the "out" provides an incentive for reckless entrepreneurial behavior, everyone knows there are many risks beyond the entrepreneur's control.

## Start-ups Come in Three Parts

Three factors make a new business successful. Every new business that grows into a large, well-established, and flourishing business is a combination of:

1. A great idea (it provides a much needed innovation)
2. The right financial backing (i.e., sufficient monetary resources)
3. The right people (the entrepreneur and the team he or she puts together)

As noted, these factors must be combined inside an envelope of complex forces that might be called risk. Successful entrepreneurs may have the great idea, the correct financial backing, and the right people to make the new start-up go, but each dimension of the new firm presents its own risks. Managing these risks successfully is the most important trait of successful entrepreneurs.

Frequently, a good idea is ahead of its time. Many aspects of various markets cannot be determined any way other than plunging in and offering a new product or service. Sometimes the entrepreneur faces a radical shift in technology that he or she could not have anticipated. Other times, a new business is started at just the wrong time in the business cycle. Starting a business is difficult in any situation, but starting one in the beginning of a recession, a turn of events impossible to foresee, may make success impossible.

Risk can be informed and reduced with information and practice. The job of public policy makers is to shape the ecosystem so that risk is more manageable and more entrepreneurs, in weighing the positive incentives against the risk of failure, try to turn their idea into a reality. And the job of education—and educators—is to make the cost of acquiring the skills that will help turn an idea into a reality less expensive. But even so, the entrepreneur must successfully manage the risks associated with the three components of any start-up: the idea, the financial backing, and the team.

## The *Actionable* Idea

The first component of a new business is the idea that motivates the entrepreneur. When thinking of a successful entrepreneur, most people envision someone with a very big idea, a breakthrough concept only a true entrepreneurial genius could conceive such as a technological innovation or discovery.

Many businesses that grow to enormous scale, however, have no radical technology at all. For example, when Bernie Marcus and Arthur Blank started Home Depot, they saw an opportunity to build a business in which economies of scale in retail hardware would pay off. Marcus took Wal-Mart's approach to selling mass market goods and applied it to one specific part of the market: hardware.

In explaining both Home Depot's and Wal-Mart's successes, people sometimes say these are in fact huge technology stories. And, up close, there is certainly tremendous technology behind each company.

Just go to a Wal-Mart, as I did in Auburn, New York, not long ago, looking for a specific item (a coffee pot in my case) that was not in stock. The departmental supervisor consulted a small inventory computer on her belt and told me the item would be restocked that very night. Sure enough, at 9:00 the next morning there were five in the store—one on display and four on the shelves just below!

Computers and a choreography of logistics make it all happen. But Wal-Mart and Home Depot, along with Target, Lowe's, Marshalls, T. J. Maxx, and the like, are so big that you could say the technology of just-in-time inventory and the logistical support it requires have been shaped by their size, not the other way around.

No matter which way you put it, it is clear that the entrepreneurs who started these companies were committed to creating a concept that would allow all of us to do a required task (in this case, buying goods for daily life) better, faster, or cheaper. Those three words—*better, faster, cheaper*—are all you need to know about the idea component of new companies.

An idea alone is not enough, however. Whether it seems far-fetched, as cell phones once did, or relatively simple (selling hardware on a massive scale), the idea must be actionable; it must be something the market values. The notion of actionable is not so much concerned with whether a human need can be accommodated with a new idea. Instead, the question is whether anyone will value—that is, be willing to spend money on—the idea if it is offered. This is the risk associated with a new product or service: Will the market pay for what you have come up with?

You could guess that cell phones would grab people's imaginations. But reorganizing the hardware business on a nationwide basis? People must have looked at Marcus and Blank as if they were nuts when they first proposed the idea of Home Depot. To Americans in the 1970s, the term *hardware store* meant the relatively cramped place on Main Street, not a sprawling megastore off the highway.

History has proven the wisdom of Sam Walton, Arthur Blank,

and Bernie Marcus's faith in the economics of the market. People value better, faster, cheaper.

No matter how affluent our society becomes, our instinct to operate rationally in the marketplace—to buy more or better for less—overrides our loyalty to neighborhood clerks and store owners who were our friends. The impersonal, the predictable (what people really see in McDonald's as they travel the country—they know the hamburger they get in Sarasota will taste exactly the same as the one they buy in Seattle), is what the American consumer wants. This is what entrepreneur Ray Kroc—who established McDonald's— understood.

Given the success of Walton, Marcus, Kroc, and Blank—men who reordered what had come before—it is worth a moment's pause to wonder if inventors like Edison and Ford—men who invented entire new industries, forever altering our ways of life in the process— are important to our society anymore. The answer is absolutely. We think that their tinkering style was of one moment in our nation's history. But that moment has been repeated so often in recent years that there is now a widely used description for these people: they work "in the garage." The reference is to the place where William Hewlett and David Packard started their company. The garage is still important. The garage gave us the video game industry. (Kids tinkering.) It gave us the software industry. (Engineers tinkering.) Tinkering remains a key part of the entrepreneurial process.

A great example comes from the Midwest Research Institute (MRI), a private nonprofit laboratory in Kansas City that in the 1950s figured out how to make the candy shell on M&M's melt in your mouth, not in your hands. Some fifty years later, the scientists at MRI are experimenting with various types of defense research and have discovered a way to detect deadly airborne microbes such as anthrax by using a new sensing technology. The breakthrough happened just as the Senate Office Building in Washington received its first letter containing lethal anthrax spores.

Overnight, a company was born: MRI spun out its invention, financed with Israeli venture capital money, and the start-up is now building machines used on Capitol Hill and many other places to inspect the nation's mail flow. Ours is a culture of tinkering.

The key to all this is what we at the Kauffman Foundation call opportunity recognition. Entrepreneurs see an unmet need and determine whether there is a way they can create a better, faster, cheaper solution to the problem. In fact, the entrepreneurial economy really begins in the search for actionable ideas. But once you have an idea, you need to do something with it. That is where the next step in our journey fits in.


## Capital: The Blood of the Entrepreneurial Firm

The old saying that you must have money to make money is true whether you are talking about investing in or starting a business. Creating a new company requires money.

One of the reasons entrepreneurial capitalism could emerge in modern America was that there was—and is—plenty of money around. It is estimated that every year $17.5 billion is invested in start-up companies. To put that number in perspective, the total budget of the Small Business Administration in fiscal year 2006 is around $600 million.

Where does all this money come from? Entrepreneurs get their money from four major sources. The first is from their own savings and funds from family and friends. This is the most important source of money because it can be readily accessed, but more importantly the application of your own money sends a signal to all the other potential sources that you take the idea seriously and have "skin in the game." If you are willing to risk your money, others are more willing to risk theirs.

The technology bubble in the late 1990s was largely fueled by venture capital, the second money source. Nearly all of the companies that were able to grow and survive—such as Google, eBay, and Expedia, just to name three—could not have come into existence and established themselves as market leaders without venture capital.

Given the high returns generated by helping to fund firms such as the ones we have just mentioned, venture capitalists have attracted so much money from investors that they no longer find it feasible to explore little deals. In this regard, because of past success, the venture capital market has really changed its stripes. It now only backs companies that are well on the path to success.

Angel funding from strangers is the third money source. It is becoming more important because venture capital funds find it harder and harder to invest in start-up companies.

In part, the federal government has emerged as the fourth money source to fill the void left by the venture capitalists. For example, the Small Business Innovation Research program (SBIR) mandates that federal agencies with budgets over $100 million set aside a minimum of 2.5 percent of their contracts for small businesses.

## Entrepreneurial Talent—People

Nothing happens in the entrepreneurial ecosystem without the entrepreneur. He or she is the risk taker, the visionary, the person who hopes not only to make himself or herself better off financially but often to improve the lot of humankind by developing a product or service that the entrepreneur *just knows* the world needs.

Who is this person? One point of this book is to suggest that it is you! Writer and philosopher George Santayana wrote: "To be an American is of itself almost a moral condition, an education and a career." To that we might add: "To be an American is also to be an entrepreneur." Most Americans have wondered at one time or another if they should start a business—that's how deeply entrepreneurship is ingrained within our character.

And the question, Should I start a business based on an insight I have, is not one of mere academic interest. Going forward, success for all of us in every walk of life will involve the identification and manipulation of innovation, whether or not we start our own companies. We cannot avoid entrepreneurial behavior—and we should not. Not only is it critical to the overall continuing success of the United States, it is part of who we are.

But entrepreneurial behavior does not have to happen inside *new* organizations. In fact, as we will see in Chapter 5, entrepreneurs inside larger firms take personal risks to instigate and manage innovation, and make the necessary changes if those firms are to continue to be competitive and indeed survive.

And while we focus on entrepreneurs who start or improve businesses, there are, increasingly, entrepreneurs in government and universities—places that in the past appeared allergic to entrepreneurs. In subsequent chapters, we will also examine the role of entrepreneurs in these institutions.

## Who Is an Entrepreneur?

What characterizes an entrepreneur? How do you know if you are one? These are complicated questions. Psychologists tell us that entrepreneurs cannot be identified on any of the standard aptitude tests. But there is something about people who become entrepreneurs. For one thing, they seem to see it in each other.

Neal Patterson, one of the cofounders of Cerner Corporation, which provides information management systems for thousands of hospitals, says that all entrepreneurs are "mutants." He means they seem different in their vision, their passion, and their energy. They are unlike regular people. They are a little crazy. I think Patterson is right to some extent.

In his book *The Hypomanic Edge: The Link Between a Little Crazy and a Lot of Success in America,* John Gartner, a professor at Johns Hopkins, says that entrepreneurs often seem driven, hyped up, almost like religious zealots. They believe they have been called to save the world and make a lot of money in the process.

In a much more scholarly book, *Exuberance,* a different Hopkins professor, Kay Redfield Jamison, describes a kind of personality that seems suited to being an entrepreneur. There are people, Jamison finds, who are perennially optimistic: to them the glass is always half full. She has observed—and so have I—that entrepreneurs think optimism leads to opportunity. (What follows from that, in my view, is that opportunity is best managed by optimists.) I think that what both Gartner and Jamison observe is very similar to what Patterson sees when he meets other entrepreneurs.

But there is still that haunting observation from psychologists: you can't determine ahead of time who will be an entrepreneur.

Many people have said to me, "I was the last person to think I had this in me."

And indeed the decision to start a company can come when you are in middle age or beyond. Harlan Sanders started Kentucky Fried Chicken (KFC) when he was sixty-five! Gary Burrell was fifty-one when he left secure employment at Allied Signal in Kansas City to help start Garmin, the company that now owns the geolocator market—every car with a map in the dash and every tank and personnel carrier in the military being guided by its satellite communications technology.

There are tens of thousands of stories just like this. In his new book entitled *If at First You Don't Succeed . . .* , longtime *New York Times* business reporter Brent Bowers studied sixty entrepreneurs and found they have certain similarities. One will certainly come as no surprise: entrepreneurs want to be in charge of their lives. In fact, some people think this is the most important variable in determining if someone will become an entrepreneur.

Ewing Kauffman, who started the foundation I work for, went off on his own because his employer tried to limit the amount of money he could make. Mr. Kauffman was very good at selling insurance and worked on commission. Eventually, he was making more than the company president, so the CEO tried to cut Kauffman's territory. Kauffman announced his resignation on the spot, famously saying that that was the last day he would ever work for anyone else.

In addition to wanting to have control over their lives, data show that a much higher proportion of entrepreneurs are dyslexic: for example, investor Charles Schwab and Kinkos founder Paul Orfalea, who recently sold his business to FedEx for $2 billion. One reason they may have started their businesses is that they found the bureaucracy inside traditional companies more frustrating than most people, since it relies so heavily on written communication.

We also know there are entrepreneurs who grow frustrated inside companies when the companies won't seize market or technology opportunities the entrepreneur sees as "no-brainers" (the opportunity recognition discussed above). Finally, Bowers tells us that most entrepreneurs share great drive and energy.

## Are Entrepreneurs Born or Made?

One school of thought says trying to foster entrepreneurship is, at its heart, just silly.

These people contend entrepreneurs are born; that is, they come out of the womb with a desire to run their own businesses. Society can provide them with resources such as education and access to capital that can make starting a business more efficient, but, these people argue, you can't create an entrepreneur. People either have the burning need to start their own businesses or they don't.

Some people who become entrepreneurs undoubtedly possess this innate drive. They are delivering newspapers by age six, babysitting and working after school as soon as their parents will allow. They are the kids who start cutting lawns at age twelve, and by the time they are thirteen, they have a lawn care service that employs their friends.

Yet simply having this drive cannot be the complete answer. We can all point to countless examples in which fifty-five-year-old government bureaucrats retire and then start companies. The 1990s downsizing turned people in their thirties and forties, who had held staff jobs all their lives, into successful entrepreneurs. In these instances, the entrepreneurial drive was not necessarily innate; in fact, many of these people will tell you that if circumstances had been different—had their organization not downsized (throwing them out of a job) or had there not been a change in political administrations (throwing them out of a job)—they would have never started their own business.

But we cannot ignore the "drive" argument. The desire to be in charge, to be your own boss, and to be the person who provides a necessary product or service is simply too common among entrepreneurs to be dismissed out of hand.

So what is it? Are entrepreneurs born or made?

This is the wrong question. The right question involves understanding how someone perceives risk. We think of starting a company as a risky business—and it is. Yet paradoxically the people who start businesses, as a rule, see it as the least risky alternative facing them at the time.

To an immigrant who comes to this country with little, starting a business is not particularly risky because he has nothing to lose. Similarly, a twenty-seven-year-old "trust fund baby" with $100 million in the bank can easily risk $10 million, $40 million, or even $80 million on a new venture. Even if he loses it all, he'll have a fortune left.

To someone in her mid-forties who has been laid off or fired, starting a new business can seem less risky than finding a new job. Either she sees the chances of finding future employment too daunting or she doesn't want to subject herself again to a situation in which she could be caught in another wave of downsizing or offshoring.

The fifty-five-year-old bureaucrat turned entrepreneur could have a different motivation. The package he receives for retiring early could be of sufficient size that he feels he can afford the risk of starting the business of his dreams.

But even if we make how they deal with risk the deciding factor in whether people become entrepreneurs, there is still one more point to be made. How people deal with risk can change over time. People willing to start a business on their own in their twenties may have very different thoughts once they reach age forty and find themselves with children to feed, clothe, and educate. Conversely, formerly risk-adverse people who suddenly find themselves with the costs of child rearing behind them may view starting a business differently once they hit their late fifties.

So the answer to whether entrepreneurs are born or raised seems to be: neither. The real question is, How does someone deal with risk at each stage of their life?

## Thinking About Entrepreneurship

This chapter has covered a lot of ground, but if there is one takeaway point, it is this: the pace of economic change is accelerating, driven by inventions, process improvements, and our perpetual quest for *better, faster, cheaper.*

Every single person in American society is caught up in this continuing economic metamorphosis, which can be disruptive. But even as it makes people feel less and less secure—Will I have a job? How can I cope with all the changes occurring around me?—the bigger picture is clear. Continuous disequilibrium brings our ultimate security. It is the entrepreneurs starting thousands of new businesses every day who guarantee that our economy will thrive. Our future depends on our continuing ability to be creative, innovative, and entrepreneurial.

---

*★ This is a letter to my son, age twenty-one, and daughter age sixteen, who are both students, in response to their question: "Daddy, how do I prepare myself for success out in the real world?" This is the same advice I offer all people in their late teens and twenties who ask me about how they should get ready for the future. ★*

---

*Kids,*

I was hoping you would ask. It's the responsibility of all parents to help prepare their children to be an economic success.

As you know, how much money you have is not the measure of your success. Ultimately, as Thomas Jefferson suggested, life is connected to the liberty to pursue happiness. And your pursuit may or may not require a lot of money.

Economic success, like happiness, is different for each person, because we all have different aspirations and hopes. And indeed you may conclude that "psychic income," the joy that comes from doing something you love, is far more important than what you earn.

Think about the places where you went to camp. Each has had only a handful of directors in its hundred-plus-year history. While being a camp director doesn't pay much, the job must present very special rewards to the people who do it, if the turnover has been that low. These directors no doubt reap significant psychic income, knowing that because of their hard work and dedication they have made the kids with whom they have worked more competent and complete humans. It's like the *Mr. Chips* movie in real life.

There is no greater reward than preparing children to be ready to absorb all the wonders of civilized life and giving them the necessary grounding so that they can contribute to or improve the world through the work they do. That is how your mother and I feel.

You should appreciate the value of family and strive to create a family supportive of your children—it is the best inheritance you can leave. The family is the source of both happiness and wealth.

All this suggests that you want to blend the right amount of income with the special sense of fit that comes from doing the things that might make you happy. This might be building bridges, coaching kids, being a journalist, making money by managing money, or being an entrepreneur and starting a business.

And that brings us to the discussion of the other kind of income—the tangible kind.

When one of you was very small, you said one of those amazingly insightful things that kids are famous for. You said that firewood was the stored-up heat of the sun. That's a perfect analogy for wealth. At the right time, it gives back the heat of hard work.

Financial wealth is created by effective (often hard) work and successful investing. To make money by working requires skills, and to make money by investing requires money. The starting point is to gain the education and expertise that permit you to become smarter, wiser, and increasingly more valued participants in labor markets. To get better jobs—not only better-paying jobs but jobs that permit you to grow—requires that you constantly become smarter, know more, and see things that need doing, making, or discovering.

Investment in your schooling and in all kinds of enriching experiences that permit you to develop a deeper context for understanding the world around you is the way in which you become equipped to enter the market ready to make wealth. Your ideas, knowledge, and ability to work are your security.

Now all of this is really a prelude to more practical advice. The question is, How should you deal with the economic world ahead of you?

Of course, you must understand it. You are entering an economy of accelerating change. I know that that is the cliché's cliché! People said it when I left college—and it was true. But there is little doubt it is truer today.

In fact, the very nature of our economic system, capitalism, has changed dramatically in the last thirty years. When I left college, a life in big business was, for many, a despised route to take. Big business was seen, with very good reason, as a stifling, noncreative environment. In the age of hippies and flower children, the thought of entering a company like General Electric, where the kind of office chair you got depended on your pay grade, was the antithesis of what we hoped life would hold. In retrospect, this was a period of economic history we can call bureaucratic capitalism.

It's different today. We now live in the most entrepreneurial time in history. In fact, we could call the current era the age of entrepreneurial capitalism. We have entered a time of continuous innovation. The United States is largely responsible for this because, though we didn't plan it, we took several steps that led to this outcome:

- We created more efficient capital markets that reward innovative companies and the people who build them.
- We invented the Internet. While it helps you guys do instant messaging, it also allows you to find almost any piece of knowledge you might need—in your work or life as a consumer—in seconds. This saves you the cost of going to the library, reading encyclopedias and specific books that might not be on the shelf or even in the building, and making phone calls to experts. Instead? Zap! You've got the information in seconds in your dorm room or at the kitchen desk.
- Most of all, through our government, we funded the growth

of universities that have made education, especially research-related graduate education, a common achievement for many.

When we began producing lots of people trained in research, in making new discoveries and expanding knowledge, we started to develop our most important asset. We have many people doing what da Vinci, Edison, Crick and Watson (who discovered DNA), and Shockley (who invented the transistor) did. In other words, millions of Americans are inventing every day, so our world continues to evolve faster and faster.

In the process of getting to this new economy, we have influenced much of the world. Many countries that have emulated our democracy have also imitated our economy. They have set up their universities the way we created ours and have copied our best business practices. Many nations have succeeded hugely as a result. Ireland is one.

When your mother and I first visited there only twenty-five years ago, it was a terribly poor country. To call home to wish your grandparents a happy anniversary required reserving the "trunk line" four days in advance! Now Ireland has the highest standard of living in all of Europe. Why? Because its new educational system offers widespread opportunity to learn about technology and science; reduced taxes have encouraged new business formation; it has built an infrastructure, including a modern phone system, roads, and airports that support innovation. All this convinced high-tech businesses, especially from the United States, to set up shop there.

By this point, you have to be wondering how all this affects you. The answer is simple but potentially a bit scary. A relatively predictable career with certain expectations of security and stability has become a thing of the past.

When *I* entered the workforce in the era of bureaucratic capitalism, you could expect big business to give you a job for life and that the government would somehow watch out for your welfare.

*You* are competing not only with American kids but also with more and more kids from other countries whose parents—just like your mother and I—have worked hard to prepare them for what is now a worldwide market for talented and skilled workers.

Today, in the era of entrepreneurial capitalism, your destiny is in your hands. Lots of American politicians think this is bad. They believe government should offer a pretty expansive safety net for all its citizens. This is a nice idea, but the more we try it, the more it appears to induce self-destructive behavior. It seems as if the human animal needs challenges to grow and contribute. Besides, the politicians' approach creates the terrible problem of what economists call the free rider—people who want the benefits of work without laboring.

But debating alternatives is a waste of time. Simply, the American dream is no longer just the *American* dream; it is the world's dream. Everyone wants to live in a growing economy with more and better consumer goods (that make up a better lifestyle). Even more important, citizens of many nations understand that the American economic formula is the basis of personal freedom. The world, already competitive, is about to become even more so.

The good news is that despite all the gloomy stuff you may hear from your professors and the complaints you hear from some businesspeople and commentators, we still have a leg up on the world in many ways. We have a skilled workforce, and we are better than most nations in making adjustments to respond to challenges. And, because our government, businesses, universities, and other institutions are already about the process of getting better in thousands of ways, we can compete more effectively.

Given all this, here are three things you should remember:

1. Never bet against the American system.
2. Know that being an American is your very best asset even as you must think of yourself as a citizen of the world or at least as a person who must succeed in a world market for talent, ideas, and skills.
3. Finally, never count on anyone but you to create your destiny.

So, you ask, "As usual, Dad, you are good at the theory, but can you tell me what to do tomorrow to help me control my future?" This time, kids, I've got some answers.

One thing should be self-evident by now. If this is an entrepreneurial economy, you had better be ready to be entrepreneurial either on your own or inside an organization that has an entrepreneurial culture. Today, most new jobs created every year are in firms less than five years old! The newest and most exciting jobs are in companies that are young. You might start one of these. It is a certainty that you will have friends who will.

But, even if you don't, you will be successful only to the extent that you can handle innovation and change. Make uncertainty your friend. See the opportunity. Get good at seeing the potential in any situation.

The second thing I'd tell you involves the person who will become your lifelong partner, your husband or wife. Many entrepreneurs I know say they could not have done it without a supportive spouse. The same goes for people who are successful in established business. Your choice of spouse is, first of all, a choice! It is the most important decision you will make, and involves a lot of risk. If it is the right choice, the returns will be extraordinary. This is the person who will make your family with you, and your family is your fortress in the world. So know your partner.

Recall the advice from Marty Head, a very successful entrepreneur herself, as well as the widow of the great entrepreneur Howard Head. Marty says your choice of a spouse should be guided by one rule: "Don't marry an idiot!"

It is good advice. It means, in the throes of starry-eyed love, be sober. Of course, if your "nonidiot" has grace and beauty, that will help. The real trait to look for is someone who is curious and will be able to grow with you. To me, your mother is the perfect role model. She is the best! She is truly supportive of my risk taking. She is independent and independently successful. This lets me learn from her more than she learns from me. Life is a long road, and you want a fully formed adult to share it with.

This advice is important from another aspect. Divorce is really upsetting to achievement, success, and the accumulation of assets, not to mention your own growth and quietude. It's worse yet if there are children, because no matter what anyone says about kids and their resiliency, a divorce is a terrible burden to impose on them.

Third, you know building a financial reserve is critical to a comfortable life. This means denying yourselves the neat things that young adults all want in exchange for the cold comfort of a bank account. Studies show that young adults who start accumulating hard assets that appreciate are able to make more risky decisions when the time comes. They know they have something to fall back on. They know they can walk out of dead-end situations. They know they can help finance a great idea if it comes along and they want to start a business.

I know we have bored you to tears with this, but this is exactly the strategy your mother and I followed. We lived "short" for a long time. We bought cheap cars (expensive wheels are the single biggest temptation for young adults) and focused our consumerism on owning our home. We were saving for your college educations before we knew you were coming.

As a result of these decisions, we didn't have to mortgage our retirement to pay for your educations. (It also permitted me to take entrepreneurial risk as a venture capital investor, and if/when I see the next big thing, I can be the initiating entrepreneur.)

Remember this lesson. When you have a family, you must sacrifice so that your children, your greatest wealth, can be on the road to accumulating their own wealth early on. It is the virtuous cycle. It pays big, but it requires discipline inside families from generation to generation.

That's it for family and personal advice.

The most important thing you can do for yourselves right now is to take in your classes as if you were preparing yourselves for a life as an entrepreneur. It is unlikely that any of your history teachers will ever talk about American history as a story of entrepreneurship. But, in fact, all of our history can be read this way. Individual risk taking is the central theme of our history. From the beginning, the notions of rugged individualism, the frontier, and manifest destiny have been part of American DNA. This makes America unique.

And, of even greater importance is the role business plays in our history. All business history is about entrepreneurship, although that is not the way your professors are likely to explain it. While they tend to see business in general—and capitalism in particular—as bad, you must remember that every penny of this nation's wealth, and the welfare that results, stems from commercial activity.

So while your professors may paint John D. Rockefeller as a rapacious capitalist, you need to understand that he leveraged new technology in ways that resulted in making American life much easier. (Incidentally, like most entrepreneurs, he saw the creation of thousands of jobs in his companies as his greatest contribution to society even though he created a foundation that has done many marvelous things.)

Fortunately, today we treat our entrepreneurs such as Michael Dell with some respect for what they do. But, read all of our history, political, cultural, and civic, as the story of entrepreneurs and understand that the underlying history of America, including the writing of the Declaration of Independence and the Constitution, is one of *creating the new*. We have been about democratizing the ways for regular people to get rich since the beginning of our nation.

You should also understand the importance of science and technology. This does not mean you need to become a scientist or an engineer. But you really must understand the logic of science and its processes in order to know how science gets into the stream of practical ideas and how it shapes commerce.

A good way to gain this understanding is to look for internships in a laboratory or in a high-technology manufacturing or engineering company. The more you can have a feel for the heartbeat of science, the more you will have a sense of the continuous nature of innovation that is the underlying genetic code of our economy.

Now for some really wild and crazy advice: practice being an inventor. We used to think that inventors were born, not made. Some are. But everyone can be much more creative with a little practice. The more you work on creating new ideas, the faster they will come.

There is a new course at Stanford jointly run by its medical and engineering schools. Four people who have just completed their undergraduate degree or a professional degree (e.g., M.D.) make a team. The team is then placed inside Stanford Hospital with the ability to go anywhere and hang around with anyone. In two months, the team must come up with three hundred ideas of how some part of the practice of medicine or the running of the hospital could be improved. This is the total immersion model of invention.

What is incredible is that the teams *always* find three hundred ways that things could be done smarter, cheaper, or faster. And they are looking in an environment where some of the smartest people already work!

What these teams go through is a process that we at the Kauffman Foundation call opportunity recognition. It is a skill that anyone can learn. The ability to see what needs exist or might exist is at the root of all entrepreneurial behavior. Once, people didn't know we needed the telephone. Cell phones, laptops, iPods, and CDs are all relatively recent inventions. The more you can hone your inventive capacity, the better able you will be to succeed in an entrepreneurial world.

Three last thoughts.

First, it is one thing to know something; it is another to act on it. People often have a reason to sell a stock but don't, then kick themselves as it falls. People know they should finish college, but they don't get around to it and look back with profound regret ten or twenty years later.

When you know you should act, when you have the necessary knowledge, then act. If you see a great idea, act! Seize the opportunity. Even if you fail, you will be more valuable to your next employer.

But knowing when to act is different than plunging ahead without sufficient thought or preparation. If you are an entrepreneur, you sometimes have to wait for the moment to bring into play your vision of what should be done. You must know when and how to act.

Second, lots of environments are not friendly to entrepreneurial people. Many big companies hunt down entrepreneurs inside their walls and fire them even though they desperately need people to act entrepreneurially. They find entrepreneurs too disruptive.

To succeed, you have to know the nuances of the environment in which you are working. You may be more productive if you are stealthlike in your approach. Bide your time. Move only when you are likely to be able to control the process. Recognize the trouble you may cause if you propose the new, the untried, or the innovative. There is an old saying, "the only people who like change are babies with wet diapers." Accept that (but don't let it stop you).

The third thing I want to tell you echoes the first thing. Your life is all about service to others. We often use the marketplace to help others, to produce a product or a service that will allow someone to do what they want to do.

The Wegmans grocery company has been called the very best company to work for in America. I was at the University of Rochester giving the commencement address in 2005 when the company's founder, Bob Wegman, who was eighty-five years old, received an honorary doctorate. His speech was profoundly simple.

He said, "When I was seven, one of the nuns who taught me said, 'Robert, you have only one job in life, and that is to get to heaven.' You know, I don't think it's too hard to get there. The secret is every time you meet someone, make sure you see what you can do for them."

I hope when you are a great success, however you choose to measure it, you can look back on a happy life of entrepreneurial success in helping others. That is a special kind of wealth. As soon as you can, you should give back to your community by giving your time or your money to your schools, to organizations that advance community welfare, to your church, and perhaps to your political party.

There is a special grace about giving, particularly when you know the trade-off: "For this much money, I could have bought a new bike, taken a vacation, bought a new car," and so on.

Every one of us has benefited from the generosity of others, people who have given of themselves or their treasure. Their gifts have helped to pave the way for you, and you should, if you can afford it, make the way smoother for someone who will come after you. You will find that this is an important part of developing the moral or ethical person you must become, someone who is not self-righteous but rather privately comfortable for having quietly paid your dues along the way.

In a strange way, this knowledge will prove a comparative advantage in many business situations.

I know you will do well.

Love,

Dad

# 5

★

## ENTREPRENEURS ARE FROM VENUS, MANAGERS ARE FROM MARS

*The emerging codependency between start-ups and big firms
and the search for common ground*

IN THE SPRING OF 2005, as the G7 finance ministers met in London to prepare for the talks scheduled for Scotland that summer, I was invited by the president of the Bank of England, Mervyn King, to a small dinner that included the heads of the central banks of Germany, China, Russia, and Canada, as well as the European Central Bank.

The conversation focused on issues relating to exchange rates, international debt, and inflation. Toward the end of dinner, our talk moved to trying to answer the question of how world economies could obtain a higher and more uniform level of growth.

After the ministers offered various ideas, most relating to the management of government budgets and international treaties on tariffs, England's chancellor of the Exchequer, Gordon Brown, asked me what role entrepreneurship played in explaining differential growth rates.

Although America is growing faster than any of the other countries except China—and has been since 2001—I sought to downplay my remarks, since I was the only American present. I talked a bit about the themes we have discussed so far in this book, stressing how entrepreneurship really is the only source of comparative advantage.

Feeling compelled to say more, however, I began to talk about public policy, pointing out a huge difference between how business and government interact in the United States and the rest of the world. When asked what I meant, there was a tailor-made explanation right at hand.

I said that only the month before, the last of AT&T had been sold. What had been the biggest company in the world—and an American business icon—no longer existed, yet nobody in American journalism, in the government, or on Wall Street thought there was anything particularly notable in its disappearance. Big companies in the United States come and go all the time; it's just something that happens rather routinely in American commerce.

Then I asked those around the dinner table if this could have happened in their countries—in France or Germany or Russia. The answer, of course, was no. Their industrial policies seek to concentrate commerce in large businesses, often controlled by dynastic families, many of which have existed since the Industrial Revolution began.

I said as long as entrepreneurs see government operating in close collaboration with a handful of giant concerns, there will be fewer new businesses. Potential entrepreneurs think—correctly— the deck is stacked against them.

Of course, I pointed out that the costly labor regulations in these countries were also hugely discouraging to entrepreneurs. (To hire an employee means that the entrepreneur/employer must commit to an extended contract—what if the hiring decision is wrong?) Worse, with their high unemployment rates (commonly over 10 percent), the risk to the entrepreneur is much greater than in the United States. If the business fails, the entrepreneur's chances of finding a job are not great.

At this point, the chancellor broke in and said, "If you want to see the next generation of French entrepreneurs, you will have to come to London!" That remark says it all.

That conversation around the dinner table tells a lot about the comparative economic advantage of the United States vis-à-vis "Old Europe." There is a bigger, more important point, however, concerning the relationship between big companies and start-ups: start-ups and entrepreneurs keep our economy growing, challenging larger firms to change.

In fact, one reason Americans have been able to look back on two decades of economic growth and success is because we allowed the forces of the capital markets to break these big firms into more efficient operating units—or, in the case of AT&T, supplant or absorb them all together. (The last of AT&T was acquired by SBC, which ironically had been one of the "baby Bells," the nickname given to the regional Bell Telephone operating companies created by the breakup of AT&T in 1981. Following the acquisition, SBC changed its name to AT&T, in order to capitalize on the equity associated with the older brand.)

It is this "creative destruction" within democratic capitalism that permits real economic growth and a continuous expansion of the pie that benefits everyone. This is not some abstract theory. It is fact. The statistics on how long big firms last in the United States speak loud and clear: throughout the 1960s and 1970s, the makeup of the Fortune 500 was remarkably stable. Turnover averaged only 4 percent, meaning that just 20 companies fell from the list (as a result of mergers, acquisitions, and closings) in a given year.

By the 1980s, the average turnover was 8 percent—or 40 companies a year—and the cumulative effect was noticeable. One-third of the firms on the list in 1980 were no longer independent entities by the time we reached New Year's Day 1990. And the pace kept moving faster. Between 1990 and 1995, some 40 percent of the Fortune 500 had fallen from the list, whether through mergers, takeovers, or failures. Of the top 100 companies on the 2005 list, nearly three-quarters had not existed on the 1980 list in their current capacity. Accordingly, of the top 100 companies on the 1980 list, only 25 still existed in 2005 in the same capacity.

What causes this amount of change? There are as many answers as there are business professors. But in the end, there are only two interrelated explanations.

The first is that there is a continuous push from underneath—that is, from recently created companies changing the nature of the market with new innovations in goods or services. In fact, many of the fastest-growing firms come into existence precisely because they have a knowledge advantage over their established competitors. The founders are often scientists or engineers who know more than anyone else about a new technology. They form their firms to exploit their innovations. As a result, they change not only the market but the competition, which is forced to try to respond to what they have.

And that brings us to the second reason for all the turnover in the American economy: it is difficult for an established firm to respond to substantial competitive threats, even though it has the money and resources to do so.

Why? Internal bureaucracy is certainly one reason. Those who work in big firms will invent countless, spurious reasons to dismiss anything that has the potential of threatening their self-interest (secure, high-paid jobs).

But, even more important, when organizations get too large, the collective nonaction of people who seek to preserve the world around them overwhelms any impulse to move rapidly or take chances, even though we have seen time and time again that the first rule of business is also the first rule of life: adapt or die.

Even so, it is the rare large firm that can communicate its goals with any clarity and then provide both the vision and the incentives for tens of thousands of employees to see that the collective goal is constantly—and dramatically—to continue to improve their product or service, always to strive to be better, faster, and cheaper than the competition, whether that competition is another established firm or some start-up in a garage overseas.

But those that can—the Procter & Gambles, the Johnson & Johnsons, the 3Ms, the IBMs (a company that survived a pitched internal battle between the visionaries and the bureaucrats), and the G.E.s—are able to survive for long times, thanks to creating a culture—carefully tended—that lets everyone know that change is part of the firm's life.

In those companies, senior management constantly communicates the seeming paradox that, for the firm to be secure, the individuals within the company must be sufficiently insecure so that they take seriously every potential competitive threat and work hard to stay substantially ahead of the pack by understanding what customers want and delivering it consistently time after time, at the very least. (In the best of all possible worlds, they introduce a product or service even before their customers know they need it.)

But, as we said, such dedication and continuous renewal are very difficult. While entrepreneurial energy can keep the effects of bureaucracy at bay for a while, eventually organizations are overtaken by the need for process and structure, a gradual hardening of the organizational arteries that accelerates rapidly once the entrepreneur/founder is no longer involved.

This contest between entrepreneurial growth and the efforts of large market-dominant firms to seek predictability as a means to self-preservation—in some cases by buying up and snuffing out the competition (Microsoft); in other cases by seeking government price protection (pharmaceuticals)—is the great leitmotif of all business theory.

Think about the life of the firm (a subject, oddly, seldom treated in business school). Companies that have achieved some scale, such as members of the Fortune 500, have growth profiles that resemble some variant of Exhibit One.

In their early years, companies experience dramatic growth and some emerge as market leaders. Inevitably, that growth slows primarily, in the opinion of Herbert Simon, who won the Nobel Prize in economics for his study of managers, because the behavior of professional managers who eventually take over the firm is different from the early entrepreneurial managers.

As Simon points out, these professional managers have a different motivation from the owner/founders. They are not driven by the need to succeed as the entrepreneurial founder was. Instead, they are content to "satisfice," in his word—that is, to be content with modest, achievable, and predictable levels of growth.

When managers satisfice, they signal to their organization that no one is to "push the envelope," "rock the boat," or "go off the ranch." These directives—all of which are just another way of saying don't take any risks—are precisely what the bureaucrats inside a firm love to hear.

As Exhibit One suggests, the satisficing strategy inevitably leads first to a slowing growth rate—there is no longer an entrepreneurial push within the organization. When it reaches the pivotal moment at which it must renew its entrepreneurial vigor in order to thrive, it refuses to take the necessary risk, and the company falters. Avoidance of risk becomes the default position. Once that hap-

## Exhibit One
## The Organizational Arc

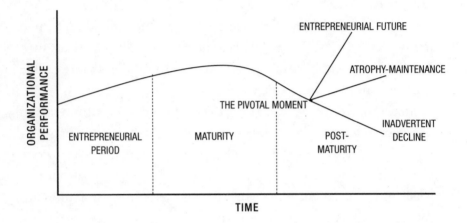

pens, death or acquisition becomes inevitable. This pattern is true in every industry.

One puzzling aspect of the life cycle of firms seems to be management's incapacity to learn from history. You would think that the first impulse inside a company when bad news hits would be to turn on the innovation afterburner. Instead, the typical first reaction is that the firm must hunker down. Many times, when it does, it never stands up again. (In Chapter 6, I explain why businesspeople are not learning from history. The reason? History is not being taught.)

It should be clear that one of management's biggest challenges is to keep the organization self-renewing, to keep its original entrepreneurial spirit. After all, every large company was once the creature of an entrepreneur. At one time, Ford Motor Company had only one employee: Henry Ford.

## Moving Toward a New Model

There is a way large companies can keep the innovative spirit alive—it involves developing a culture that treats the making of strategy as a never-ending process, one that involves as many of the people in the firm as possible. But before we discuss that in detail, let's see why continuing on the traditional path is exactly the wrong way to go.

The conventional wisdom can be stated simply: you can be one of two types if you run a company. There are visionaries who are distinguished for their entrepreneurial talents and there are managers.

In fact, in the world of venture capital, there is an axiom that says entrepreneurs can seldom manage growth. The belief among venture capitalists is let the entrepreneur start the business, then move him or her aside once the company begins to experience scale growth. Then a manager is needed. Boards of directors take a similar view. Every day, a board member calls a head-hunting firm and says one of two things: "For our next president, we need an entrepreneur-type person who can see the future," or, "We think the firm has had enough vision for now, so we need a manager to put Joe's wonderful ideas to work for the company."

This situation always gives the new manager a fifty-fifty chance of getting it wrong! This is unacceptable. An executive who can manage growth but is incapable of dealing with growing complacency within the organization and the threats that can come from outside is bound to fail. At moments when a company needs to change course, to make new bets, to take risks to survive, a conventional manager is not the person to lead the reinvention or redirection needed for recovery.

Conversely, an entrepreneurial manager, one who focuses all of

his energy on increasing revenues and earnings, will not pay sufficient attention to creating the necessary procedures to make sustaining that growth possible. But that takes us full circle. As we have
seen, stable growth cannot happen without nearly continuous renewal of the organization. Companies must respect and encourage
the intrusions and challenges that entrepreneurial employees bring
as part of the dynamic within the firm. It is clear that we need a
new model to make that possible.

What should this new model look like? It is all well and good to
say we will start with a completely blank piece of paper as we go
about creating a new model that will allow entrepreneurial capitalism to flourish, but that is not entirely realistic.

No matter what kind of model we build, it must accommodate
the three forces that shape any business: (1) the structure and incentives in the capital market at any moment; (2) the nature and speed
at which technological innovation is emerging; and (3) the stock of
human capital—that is, the talent—available to operate firms. These
three factors are the dynamic constants of the market: they always
have and always will describe the totality of the business environment (see Exhibit Two).

Every business is influenced by the ways in which these forces
move and interact with each other. We need to take that into account as we outline the following objectives we want the organization to accomplish going forward. Specifically:

- The culture of the new corporate model must be
  characterized by continuous and purposive change.
- It must be well-run and growth oriented.
- It must compete in markets that have more and more
  technology, employing technology to reduce costs and
  help companies stay ahead of the competition.

## Exhibit Two
## Future Resource Set That Defines Future Moments

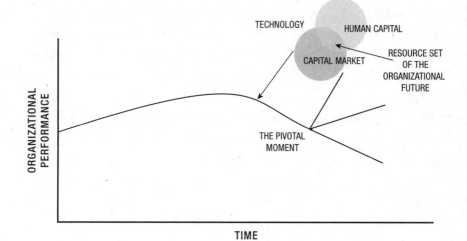

- It must recruit and develop innovative and technically adept people and create an environment where their creative activity is maximized.
- It must satisfy the needs of the capital markets.

When you look at those bullet points, you realize the new operating model must master three variables.

Capital markets seek size as a proxy for predictable returns. Bigger firms have more command of their markets and thus higher margins. Technology requires capital for its development and/or adoption of each new breakthrough. The scale of the technology is important, because the greater the scale, the less the unit cost. The first copy of a new version of Windows costs Microsoft billions of dollars to produce; the one millionth copy, just pennies. And, in the end, the human factor is not only responsible for the turns and surprises that technology development presents but also required for successful financing and commercialization.

Clearly, each of these three factors is vital. But in the end, the size and the creativity of the innovative population is the most significant determining factor of what the life cycle of firms will be. Unless the corporation is filled with creative people, it is not long for this world.

So the new corporate model must accommodate the demands to deploy capital in larger and larger units while factoring in that the generative capacity of entrepreneurial organizations requires integration around human talent. That last phrase presents an important clue.

The bias toward larger firms, as we have noted throughout, in part sprang from the economies of scale that big firms can produce, and in part because of the safety that presumably came with their size. ("General Motors cannot fail." Or, "General Motors will not be allowed to fail—the implications for the economy would be too profound.") Such statements, once a given in the American conversation, no longer are as we watch many of the largest firms—General Motors being one of them—struggle with trying to explain to the market why they should continue to exist.

At the moment, numerous large firms—Microsoft and Pfizer to name just two—appear powerless to expand their value in the stock market. The market is signaling that bigger is not necessarily better, which is easy to understand. The message of what a large company's mission is or what its value proposition is over the entire scope of its operations is hard to explain to the legion of individual investors, let alone hundreds of thousands of workers employed by such an organization.

All of this suggests that human capital might be organized into smaller units where output is maximized, a situation in which we have a constellation of smaller organizations making up one corporate entity. CEO Jeff Immelt's strategy in the post-Welch era is to break G.E. into smaller units that operate as independent entrepreneurial entities. Similarly, IBM is inventing new companies within its corporate structure to develop some of the firm's best new ideas so returns can be maximized outside of the company's main gravitational force. And Johnson & Johnson continues to operate like a holding company for purposes of marketing and access to capital markets, but it is really a family of much smaller interrelated firms.

As this trend continues, it will become easier for investors to analyze the relative efficiency of companies. As a result, the inclination of capital markets to force continued agglomeration of firms into bigger and bigger entities may no longer prevail. As information becomes less costly and more accurate and as comparable situations become easier to assess (making it easier to assess risk), we are likely to see increased tension over the size of firms. It may turn out that investment capital may produce higher returns by supporting the development of new firms spun out of older, larger ones; that is, capital may find that smaller is better.

It could be that in a world where there may be too much capital, there will be competing forces at work that make the outcome in the next ten years hard to predict. Simple efficiency may continue to favor larger companies. However, it may be that the returns in these companies cannot compete with those consistently coming from an ever-increasing number of entrepreneurial firms. Assuming that government will not enforce an industry policy that favors large firms, and if large firms cannot become creative fast enough to compete with entrepreneurial firms, capital will continue to chase smaller firms.

## Where Large Companies Went Wrong

As we have seen, the key to success in the economic ecosystem of entrepreneurial capitalism is balancing the mix of human capital, ideas, and financial capital. When we consider the problem of the apparent lack of entrepreneurial behavior in large firms, it appears that they have let the forces of the capital market prevail to the long-term detriment of the firm.

Research and development (R&D) serves as a case in point. Convinced that they are unable to convert the breakthroughs they have discovered into usable products—to use just one known example, Xerox scientists spawned much of the personal computer revolution through their discoveries, which other companies capitalized on—large companies are increasingly outsourcing their research function. The days of big R&D spending are over because the capital markets won't tolerate the inefficiencies. And there is no end of experts who suggest that this is the only way to go. I fall into this camp—sort of.

It is clear that outsourced research can be more efficient and reduce investment risk, while providing incentives for start-ups to concentrate in this area both in the hopes of making a profit and possibly getting acquired. But another dimension to the problem keeps me from being a full-blown convert. Our largest companies have such enormous distributional and manufacturing capacity that they cannot strictly rely on finding innovation outside their walls. That is why the symbiosis between big companies and start-up high-tech firms must emerge and be encouraged. As technological innovation and the speed of emerging technology increases, larger companies must be fully conversant with the state of all research and innovation, and indeed they should be contributors to the underlying field.

Companies such as 3M, Boston Scientific, and EMC prosper by remaining committed to internal research. But their ability to strongly fund internal innovation springs from their ability to demonstrate to investors that there will be substantial returns. Investors appreciate the internal culture of the firm and its strategic view, but they wouldn't if economic returns were not forthcoming. If investors specifically, and the capital markets in general, are not confident that the rewards of investing in research won't outweigh the risks, they will be reluctant to fund it.

This just points out how ironclad the rules of financial markets are. Even in a period of surplus capital, the deployment of capital is still dependent on the calculations of risk premiums. Money will always tend to seek the highest, safest return. And, in times of transition—such as now as we move from one type of economy to another—it is hard to make rational decisions on what will happen in the long term.

The key here—as it was when we talked about the right corporate size for organizing—is to find a middle ground between big and small companies. The question, of course, is how.

As we think on all these themes, it becomes more and more evident that it is the manager who creates the successful entrepreneurial organization. If we are to have an economy in which startups and existing large companies become similar or symbiotic or both, to make our system of emerging entrepreneurial capitalism more successful, we must have managers in both groups who understand the needs and culture of the other.

Those who operate large concerns must appreciate the risks that the nascent firm faces and (if successful) what the entrepreneur has accomplished. More than a theoretical knowledge or an empathetic response, the large company manager must appreciate the culture of freedom, creativity, and precision of judging in ambiguous circumstances (when there is no financial cushion to protect the continued life of the firm from bad decisions) that characterize the start-up phase of any business.

In turn, the entrepreneur must appreciate both the cultures that are in many ways forced upon big companies by their history, and the pressures they face from capital markets and, increasingly, the government. But perhaps the most difficult task for the entrepreneur is to grasp why leaders of large firms have been trained so differently. In our economy, in which the sheer scale of many firms is hard to comprehend, investors are more confident in people whose skills involve the management of complex organizations.

This mutual appreciation is not going to be easy, as simply talking about one common phrase will show. *Managing by the numbers* means two completely different things to entrepreneurs and to managers in large firms. In the first instance, it means getting the firm through the next payroll or stretching the investors' commitment to some scheduled goal or milestone—for example, when a new compound has passed the next FDA hurdle in the process of being approved for the markets. To managers in large firms, managing by the numbers presumes a level of ongoing operations and continuous study of the metrics that chart the progress of the business.

One practical way to think about the difference is to imagine the concept of passion among investors in giant companies and in start-ups. Few people know someone who is passionate about her ownership interest (say, 3,000 shares) in G.E. It is hard for an investor to feel confident in knowing what the company really does—jet engines, power generation, financial services, plastics, medical imaging, information, and entertainment. The company is just too big to get a handle on. And even if we were to say that the real focus of the investor's confidence is the company's leading role in producing jet engines, the rational investor cannot wax poetically regarding the wonder and quality of such machines or in her infinitesimal ownership stake.

In contrast, a venture capitalist can fall into a rapture regarding the prospects of a company with a new software-based product that can detect, say, traces of explosive compounds that a hypothetical terrorist might carry on his or her person.

So the reality is that managers and entrepreneurs have a hard time appreciating the other's history, ways of thinking, and pressures that each faced from the market and investors. And yet, in the years ahead, they will both face a similar problem: how to anticipate a future in which the interaction and integration of the innovations and capability of both types of firms is hugely more fluid.

In fact, it is likely that as capital markets evolve, as risk is handled with greater and greater efficiency, and as technology continues to develop at rates that overwhelm large firms, we might be close to a period in which large firms become smaller with greater frequency through strategic devolution strategies. And, as we appreciate from the experience of the last two decades, smaller firms can grow into enormous organizations in a very short period of time, only in some cases to begin to shrink in order to better serve their customers.

Going forward, the modern firm will have to adapt to the appropriate scale size with great speed, or else it will utilize capital inefficiently and be unable to capture and exploit technological opportunity effectively. To achieve these ends, firms at both ends of the development spectrum—large and established and small start-ups—face a similar challenge. They must create and implement strategy faster and more effectively.

Thus, thinking about the common ground between start-ups

and established firms, the focus must be on how the firm's leadership thinks about the entrepreneurial challenge facing the company regardless of its size. Indeed, the challenge is nothing short of an imperative. No big company manager or small company owner has the option not to engage in continuous strategy making to meet the changing demands of the market.

## The Fourth Conversation

Managing within a system of entrepreneurial capitalism requires firms of both sizes to be continuously engaged in strategy considerations. All businesses engage in three discussions. First, they worry about their customers and the direction of movement among their customers' needs and tastes. This is the sales conversation.

Second, every company, no matter what its size, worries about its capacity to please its customers and to win more customers. This is the production/logistics conversation.

Third, every company engages in a continuous discussion regarding its financial resources. Without the ability to make money by selling at more than the cost of goods or services sold, the company is out of business. This internal discussion also looks at whether the company possesses sufficient capital and debt capacity to remake its future.

To those three conversations that occur in business every day, we must add a fourth: as the future unfolds, the issue of strategy will take on much greater importance.

We are reaching a point of constant innovation. Unlike past periods in which innovation was a herky-jerky process, coming in compressed lumps of time, now we enjoy a continuous flow of innovation. Not only is the velocity of technological change increasing in every industry, but the lines between where the technology is best applied are blurring. Thus, the strategy problem is more and more intense. As a result, there must be a *fourth conversation* inside every organization that is as ubiquitous as the other three.

In many established firms, strategy is a once-a-year meeting involving senior staff only. The discussion is often held at a resort where strategy is the topic in the morning—usually with outsiders being brought in to give their perspective of what is going on in the business universe—and sports, often golf, is the pastime in the afternoon. In this environment, strategy is necessarily thought of as a discrete event, with no one—except perhaps the CEO—owning the outcome.

In contrast, the fourth conversation presumes that strategy is a constant discussion, taking place throughout the organization on an ongoing basis. This approach creates a continuous strategy dialogue characterized by three elements.

First, for the delegation of strategic decision making to be truly effective, management must absolutely articulate the goals of the company. But these goals should be presented as just the general direction of the company, with the understanding that management will make continuous adjustments to capture new opportunities as well as deal with various threats and challenges. These adjustments must be openly discussed throughout the organization as they are made.

Opening up the process is the right way to go. Today, when there is continuous technology development, it is folly to expect that just one person can accumulate all the facts that will yield the appropriate insight. By distributing strategy on a continuous basis company-wide, the CEO and senior managers gain more perspective; they deal with people who (a) are closer to the marketplace and (b) have differing perspectives about what needs to be done. And since this process is iterative, the company can move faster, decreasing its chances of being blindsided by rapid changes in the marketplace.

There is an added benefit. If people are empowered within the context of a general strategic framework, the commitment and ownership of the firm's strategy is much more widely established. When the phrase *the firm's strategy* is uttered, many people hear *my strategy*.

The benefit of this approach is clear. Instead of strategy being an annual discussion involving a limited number of players who hope to come up with ideas that will please the chief executive and the board, we have a system in which a wide range of observers are empowered and rewarded for strategic insight and judgment. This is, of course, what the best small companies do.

Second, the fourth conversation helps create a new type of manager. To engage in continuous, widely distributed strategy discussions requires a manager different than the one produced by our nation's business schools. The success of entrepreneurial capitalism depends on the creation of the *entrepreneurial manager,* someone who, through training inside a company, learns the skills of both an effective manager and a successful entrepreneur.

For the American economy to move forward, the creation of this dual manager is essential. If historically, entrepreneurs were gun-toting cowboy types (from Mars) and big company managers were deliberate, cool, and calculating types (from Venus), the modern manager must be from, and ready to work on, Earth with a combination of skills that are risk taking and rational all at the same time.

It is becoming common for entrepreneurs to sell their firms to larger competitors that hope to obtain entrepreneurial managers and culture along with the acquisition. Likewise, many entrepreneurial start-ups, anticipating their eventual life as big firms themselves, seek executives who have worked inside larger companies to ensure that their start-up obtains the culture and systems they need to satisfy their customers as the firm grows. In short, they are each looking for the skills found inside the other. That's why both need to have dual, or entrepreneurial, managers.

The entrepreneurial manager must be both the visionary and the consolidator. Most people say those skills are incompatible; you are either one or the other. But there are few facts to support that assumption, which probably stems from the way most businesses have been run until now.

For example, people with Master of Business Administration (MBA) degrees are not commonly found inside entrepreneurial firms. Most MBAs are hired by consulting firms where, even if they are working on corporate strategy, they do so in a highly mechanical or mathematical way. Nothing inside the culture of these organizations prepares the MBA for the intuitive decision making that characterizes the entrepreneur. In fact, this kind of decision making is usually disparaged by the business school curriculum, and yet the decisions that result tend to be sound, since the people making them have learned to trust their judgment.

Here's another example of why the common thinking that you are either an entrepreneur or a manager is wrong. Consider where most managers get their education.

Two institutions vie for being the most common alma mater of chief executives of the companies that make up the Fortune 500. It probably won't surprise you that Harvard is one. The other: the University of Wisconsin.

Wisconsin has always been known as the single largest producer of college faculty in the nation, a population that by and large seeks to distance itself from the world of business. And indeed most of the population views the university as having an antibusiness bias. So I asked John Wiley, a successful entrepreneur who has been a professor of engineering at Wisconsin and is now the school's chancellor, what accounts for the fact that Wisconsin produces so many CEOs.

His answer was twofold: (1) the university has for years implicitly encouraged student leadership in every single undergraduate and (2) the culture of the school promotes a sort of quiet competence. His explanation makes a lot of sense. To go to the University of Wisconsin is to experience a sense of immediate adulthood imposed by the expectations of a respected and caring faculty. The school's administration seems invisible. Indeed, students can imagine that they run the place—and it is true in many ways.

The students legally own both daily newspapers. Those papers are independent and have been for decades. The students own the student union, the sailboat fleet, and many other parts of the university. It is common for students to have to act as executives. At the same time, there is never anything made of this. If you go to the university's Web site or take your kids there to visit, never will anyone even recognize this aspect of university life.

The fourth conversation focuses on developing the dual manager who is entrepreneurial yet aware of the need to build structure. And these are the kinds of skills students seem to gain at the University of Wisconsin.

The future is only secured by the execution of the right strategy today. This dialectic between preparing the firm for the future and making the present conform to this vision must be done throughout the entire organization, and that requires a special kind of manager.

Former General Electric CEO Jack Welch was fond of saying he didn't need people trained as MBAs. He said the best system for GE would be for business schools, through their admissions process, to find people who would be good at business, then send them to General Electric without spending a day at the business school itself. That is where they would receive the best training for managing in the entrepreneurial economy.

Welch possessed a keen understanding of the need for clearly articulating an overall objective ("we will either be first or second in a market, or get out") then delegating the creation of the strategy that would achieve the objective. Although he never put it this way, Welch was running a school for dual managers where they were trained as both visionaries and operating managers. General Electric under Welch did a great deal to show that big companies could be entrepreneurial. The executives he trained now run many of America's most successful and entrepreneurial businesses.

The fourth conversation requires managers to think of the business world as a symbiotic web comprised of both new and established firms. It rests on the premise that neither is better, but both are needed to strengthen and resolve the future of the other in a world where barriers among industries are falling as new technologies create wholly new fusions of talent and capital.

A final element of the fourth conversation is that it cannot tolerate bureaucrats. In fact, a central tenet is that bureaucracy needs to be rooted out and destroyed in large part because it generates people who are openly resistant to change.

## Looking at the Situation Differently

By seeing the future of corporations as being driven by the need to become and remain increasingly entrepreneurial, we see the tension between start-ups and established firms. One is entrepreneurial in everything it does in its early stages of growth. The other stands as an example of what an entrepreneurial firm can morph into. As we have seen, there is a desperate need to find common ground, to fit our new form of capitalism.

The industrial economy was structured around capital investment and technology. The human side of the equation was to supply labor and some management in a relatively stable strategic environment where monopoly and quasi-monopoly conditions characterized many markets.

Entrepreneurial capitalism stands on a different premise. Individuals who are highly educated and ready to undertake risk have shouldered the weight of sustaining the economy. These entrepreneurs—as creators of new companies and as agents for change inside established ones—will propel an entirely different economic identity for the firm.

Many modern large firms exist without factories or enormous back offices. Examples include software firms such as Microsoft and Oracle and firms built on applications (eBay and Google). IBM tells us in its ads that it is a consulting company, and, in fact, the majority of its revenue is now derived from selling IBM's experts' time. This is the new corporation—people and ideas. Financial capital is less and less important.

And this represents a major change. Many corporations, even new start-ups, do not need great amounts of cash. In fact, many "people companies" develop their own cash surpluses. In 2004, Microsoft returned $75 billion to shareholders in the form of a dividend—cash the company had no foreseeable need of.

The assets in these firms are not factories or machinery—they are people, or more specifically the ideas in the heads of very creative people. The law has developed elaborate mechanisms to define and protect what is called intellectual property. The view is that the unique sets of ideas that underlie the products and services sold by "people companies" should be given a separate legal life.

But with the coming of Linux and other open software approaches, in which the intellectual property is turned over to the community of users, the idea of property is less and less clear. IBM is becoming an open collaboration company. It is making many of its patents available for others to exploit through a treaty in which the company shares in collaboration. It increasingly sees its future as a cooperative competitor.

Universities (discussed in the next chapter) may begin to rethink their position that ideas developed at the university belong to the university. Year in and year out, four universities report more patents and more revenue than any others: Stanford, the University of California–Berkeley, Massachusetts Institute of Technology, and the University of Wisconsin. Yet these universities have the most open attitude about letting faculty exploit whatever they discover.

But instead of these four universities sacrificing money, they seem to be benefiting. These schools receive far and away much larger gifts from alumni and successful faculty than the income other universities receive from holding on to the inventions created at their schools.

These four universities see themselves as akin to open corporations, sharing information and prospering from the strength of the social networks and shared competencies that they make available at critical stages of an idea and a business's development.

When all these developments are considered together, it may be that the corporation of the future is really an open "commons" with its ability to prosper dependent on the people who congregate within the organization and how well they work together as a team to exploit ideas. The notion of assets will reduce to the skill of the organization's social network and the competency of the group to make money by selling its ideas and their application faster and better than competitors to whom the basic concepts and ideas are available.

In a recent speech in Sydney, Australia, Rich Newton, dean of the College of Engineering at UC–Berkeley, told the story of a colleague who helped him realize that the San Francisco/Berkeley/Oakland Bay Area is itself a virtual corporation.

This is not such a far-fetched idea. England, in part because of London's concentration of corporations and people needed to run them, became the most powerful nation in the eighteenth century. New York played an equally critical role as it displaced London as the world's financial center. Doing business in contemporary New York provides many "free" goods including immediate access to all the supporting firms, all the experts, and all the infrastructure to operate a worldwide trading or banking firm. The Bay Area, like New York and London, really is a metacorporation. And, while in time, the importance of immediate proximity may diminish as a result of the Internet, it may be that the opposite comes to pass. We may find that individual creativity is much enhanced when people join functioning teams that have come together to solve problems.

The entrepreneurial economy is forcing the future upon us—and upon the way companies both large and small will be structured. Companies of every size will look more and more like a team of people creating and exploiting ideas. We may well be on our way to a vision in which the size of the firm (really the optimal culture of teams working together) is continuously balanced with intellectual productivity and the ability to take innovations to the market.

## What the Corporation of the Future Might Look Like

Envisioning a new dynamic between big companies and start-ups is the central task for business leaders and policy makers if our economy is to continue to expand and become even more productive.

The starting point is an understanding that the relationship will continually evolve; that is, the relationship today is more complicated than one in which the big company merely buys smaller companies, hoping to gather up new technology to push through its much larger production and distribution infrastructure.

To be effective, companies both big and small must develop at least four characteristics:

1. An entrepreneurial culture that is embedded in the firm's strategy.
2. An understanding of the interrelationship between financial capital, emerging technology, and human capital.
3. An understanding of the importance or nonimportance of scale.
4. A new view that requires managers to be competent in *both* large and small organizational behavior.

---

★ *I recently received this letter at the Kauffman Foundation:* ★

---

*Dear Dr. Schramm,*

*I know all about the foundation's good works and your view that our economy is moving toward what you call entrepreneurial capitalism.*

*But I've just lost my job as a middle-level manager with a company I've been with for eighteen years. They closed our local operation and moved what we did offshore. I'm fifty. What am I to do?*

*Sincerely,*

*Stanley S. Smith*

*P.S. I don't want to move overseas.*

---

★ *Here is my response.*

*It may help all of us in middle age (and beyond) to think about how we want to plan our economic future.* ★

---

*Dear Mr. Smith,*

I was so sorry to hear you lost your job. I am honored you should ask my advice.

The changes in the economy you have heard me talk about are happening around the world, not just here at home. And those shifts are directly related to what happened to you—and how you should respond.

First, don't despair. For more than a decade, many other people your age and in your position have been experiencing what you have just had happen. But you haven't been reading about a crisis in midcareer unemployment. There is a reason for that. Our economy is absorbing folks like you who have been (temporarily) caught as we transition from one phase of the economy to the next.

While this transition is profound, it is playing out in a way that is actually making our economy stronger. That means the chances are excellent that you will not only find another position but also find one that is both equally (or more) fulfilling and at a (hopefully) higher rate of pay—if you use this time between jobs to prepare yourself for the balance of your career.

While it doesn't feel like it to you right now, the fact that our economy continues to evolve is a good thing. The automobile industry produced more jobs than the horse and buggy age ever did, and today's technology-based environment will create far more employment than traditional manufacturers ever could have dreamed of, even when their factories were running flat out in the 1950s.

Critics complain that eBay and Amazon have driven independent retailers out of business. But if you look closer, you will see that half a million eBay users are full-time vendors—selling through the site is their sole occupation. Similarly, many products purchased on Amazon's Web site are from independent sellers—the only connection to Amazon is the use of the site. So little independent stores still exist. But now, instead of just serving customers who walk down Main Street, they are able to sell worldwide.

Just one other thought before I offer some pragmatic suggestions. It is useless to think about what happened to you as somehow the fault of your former employer or a shortcoming of the political process. Belonging to a union would not have protected you for one hour longer. To vastly oversimplify, what happened to you is a result of many companies in other countries (successfully) imitating what has made the United States successful.

After studying the American economic system, countries and companies around the globe now understand the key to a strong economy is innovation. And with so many companies worldwide now practicing what I call entrepreneurial capitalism, *every business everywhere* must evolve faster than ever before—whether that means discovering new products or processes more quickly, or finding more innovative and less expensive ways to do business.

We really don't want to take the steps that could stop this. We could, of course. We could erect tariff barriers to keep our jobs "onshore," but the result would be counterproductive.

Many of the goods we use every day are as cheap as they are because they are made overseas by much more efficient companies. This makes our cost of living much lower, and it actually helps you right now as you go through your transition, because lots of the things your family needs are far less expensive than they would be if they were made in the United States.

If we imposed tariffs on foreign goods, prices here at home would rise dramatically. Even worse, other countries would retaliate by refusing to buy the enormous amount of goods we export.

So the risk of imposing tariffs—which on the surface looks like a way to keep jobs here at home—is extremely high. It could lead to a worldwide recession, throwing millions out of work for an extremely long time. The net result? You would still be out of a job, and your future would be much bleaker.

So don't be bitter. There is no time for bitterness, and really no one is at fault. Think about it this way: you are ahead of many other people who will have no choice but to go through what you are now experiencing.

The economic transition I just described is permanent. You need to begin with that fact as you plan and manage the next phase of your career.

*Here's the most important single piece of advice, I can offer: you should approach this next stage of your working life as if you were an entrepreneurial company in start-up mode. You need to plan how to enter the market and make sure your value is seen by your customer (your new employer), recognizing that the new employer could very well be you.* Our donor here at the Kauffman Foundation, Ewing Kauffman, had a favorite aphorism: "Make a job: don't take a job." You now possess the opportunity to make that a reality.

But even if you again opt to work for someone else, you will need to take the entrepreneurial mindset you have developed into your new job. In an entrepreneurial economy, entrepreneurial behavior is both valued and essential. Valued, because the skills associated with entrepreneurship— being able quickly to analyze and react to information; being self-reliant and having a thorough understanding of your market—will be the price of entry, no matter what you do in the years ahead. Necessary, because you will be doing this again at least once, more likely twice, if you work until you are sixty-five. Currently, people change jobs, on average, almost every four years. This tells you that you have to be continuously attractive to a labor market that is continuously evolving.

And this means you have to be constantly learning—that is, gaining skills that will make you more valuable to future employers—no matter how the economy evolves. That's an important point. Given how fast the economy is changing, it is tempting to try to guess what will be the next growth industry and to try to tailor your skills for that sector. The world-wide business landscape is evolving too fast for you to try to be that specific. You should analyze where the world is going in general; that is, bet on a bigger technology component in whatever your next job is, not on what specific kind of hardware will be the standard, and go from there. Determine what your talent is (not necessarily your skills or your experience!) and retool.

I will give you surprising advice about where you can turn for help: there is a lot to be learned at community colleges. Nearly one-third of community college students already possess some form of post secondary degree or certificate. In addition, some of the for-profit universities have courses geared to the more pragmatic skills sought by the market.

Even if you have graduate training from a respected university, these places are wonderful for picking up the trail of what's new. Also, read trade publications. The articles talk about what is current. They're a great way to refocus your talent and self-learning. (And, of course, these periodicals often have job postings that explain just what future employers are looking for.)

But learning new skills will only take you so far. Flexibility, especially mental flexibility, will be required for success in the workplace in the years ahead.

Here's a story from real life. A man I know in Kansas City lost his job as a construction foreman for a large and successful builder. As the company's pool of general laborers began to be populated by Spanish-speaking immigrants, the company strongly and repeatedly suggested to the foreman that he learn Spanish and offered to pay for lessons. The foreman outright refused—and was fired.

No doubt he thought the immigrants needed to speak English (and many do), and not surprisingly he blames them for the fact that he lost his job. As simple as it is, this story tells everything.

When a construction foreman in the heartland must learn Spanish to stay employed, the lesson could not be clearer. Every job is changing. Everyone must grow and develop new skills constantly. (Notice, too, the immigrants were willing to come to the United States in search of a better life. Part of the flexibility I talked about could involve moving, as much as you are reluctant to relocate.)

If the unemployed foreman takes three months during his hiatus from the job market and learns enough Spanish to be effective at leading construction laborers, he will have his old job back or a better one overnight!

How many times in a coffee shop have you heard a gaggle of retirees talking endlessly about how things were at their former company? You can't be one of those guys who look back on work situations with nostalgia. Things are moving too fast.

You need to be looking ahead. Lots of self-help books talk about the business of reinventing ourselves. It is good advice.

I think your only way back into the workforce and the only way you will be able to keep up with the changing economy in the years to come is if you take the message of reinventing yourself deeply to heart. This means more than simply changing your aspirations. To reinvent yourself means acquiring the new knowledge and new skills we talked about earlier. That, coupled with a new view about how you are connected to the labor market and how the U.S. labor market is connected to the global and increasingly entrepreneurial economy, will make you much more prepared to take your place in the new world.

The next question is, How do you tell the world you are ready?

Begin by preparing a résumé. I've talked to many people who believe—and often have been told—that once you get your résumé just right, the battle is won. You send it out and wait for the world to beat a path to your door.

*Wrong!*

First, you do not have just one single résumé. Your résumé should tell your story differently in different situations. Remember, you have to be entrepreneurial in the entrepreneurial labor market. See the opportunity and speak to it. Not all opportunities are the same.

To oversimplify, if you are applying for a job with a marketing company, stress your marketing skills. Do you want to work for a technology company? Highlight your computer/engineering background.

Don't begin with a bunch of platitudes about how you seek meaningful work. Say that you want to *contribute* to the growth, innovation, and fullblown success of the employer. Present yourself as someone the company desperately needs, not someone who views work as some kind of leisurely journey of self-fulfillment.

As you go about your entrepreneurial approach to selling yourself, you might decide you want to become an actual entrepreneur, the founder of a start-up business. This is very common for people in your position.

Let me tell you another story. Back in the 1980s, San Diego suffered a huge shock with the aerospace industry cutbacks. The newspapers wrote endlessly about the rising numbers of jobs lost through downsizing. The whole town was abuzz with talk of a bleak economic future.

But a funny thing happened on the way to the inevitable economic meltdown. It never happened. In fact, San Diego is now one of the fastest-growing and most affluent parts of America.

Why? Well, as aerospace companies displaced engineers, hundreds of them decided to develop their pet ideas into new companies. They became entrepreneurs. They made their next job and many more.

The urge to start a business when out of a job is not limited to engineers. In every recession, tens of thousands of people who lose their jobs start businesses. In fact, it is the surest way for the American economy to climb out of a recession. It is one of our secret economic ingredients to a more stable economy.

This is your time to experience, participate in, and help form the entrepreneurial economy. Do not pay much, if any, attention to the daily press: when it comes to economics, the press seldom gets anything right. Keep focused on the future. Reinvent yourself so that you can become a contributing player to the continued growth and expansion of someone else's business or your own.

The result? I will bet you can look forward to a bright future that you help to make.

Our new entrepreneurial society and the changes it has created have given you more power than ever before to shape your future. Take advantage of it.

I wish you great success!

Regards,
Carl J. Schramm

# 6

★

## UNIVERSITIES AND THE ENTREPRENEURIAL IMPERATIVE

*The singular destiny of higher education*

OUR COLLEGES, universities, and business schools should be at the very heart of entrepreneurial capitalism as the biggest contributors to the changing economic landscape. But they are not. They have been taken off course by:

- Graduating degreed people who are not educated and who are certainly not as prepared as they need to be to contribute;
- Becoming too bureaucratic, and bureaucracy is the antithesis to entrepreneurial capitalism;
- Confusion about their mission; and
- The fact that they don't even teach very well.

Instead of aiding economic change, they are in many cases a hindrance, which is one of the greatest ironies of our age. Many—if not most—of our great universities were founded by entrepreneurs and were intended to be entrepreneurial in their own right, but they have not turned out that way.

In summing up the state of American higher education in the latter part of the twentieth century, historian John Thelin could only conclude that

> American colleges and universities have wandered into a state of continual expansion characterized by overextension of functions without clarity of purposes, a pattern that has fostered administrative bloat and other spending excesses. . . . The ambiguity and uncertainty displayed in recent years with respect to societal roles indicates a drift in mission and character.

Let's examine how universities lost their way, and more important, what can be done to make sure they return to their roots to support the entrepreneurial imperative.

## Universities Were Always Entrepreneurial

The modern university is the most important institution ever devised. The scientific method and democracy itself can trace their roots back to the ancient prototype of the university: the Academy of Plato and Aristotle. There is little doubt that the American university represents the highest development of the idea, and as we shall see, was a propulsive force in our nation's advancement.

Two early manifestations of the modern American university were started by the entrepreneurs John D. Rockefeller (University of Chicago, founded 1890) and Leland Stanford (Stanford University, 1891), who knew research was the key to America's future. But the tradition goes back even further. Ben Franklin, in shaping what became the University of Pennsylvania, proposed that the school focus on "practical instruction." It would not pursue learning and knowledge as ends in themselves but would cultivate "an inclination, joined with an ability, to serve mankind, one's country, friends and family."

From the beginning, our universities were incredibly entrepreneurial, placing a heavy emphasis—especially in the sciences—on coming up with immediate solutions to the nation's problems. A transformative step in this process—both in terms of making higher education readily available and setting direction—was the Morrill Act of 1862, which provided grants of federal land in each state as the basis for endowing state universities. The act prescribed that the new universities focus on practical subjects such as agriculture, engineering, and military science.

These land-grant universities, as they became known, quickly established themselves as substantial research entities, and the scope and scale of both their research and teaching quickly led to their being counted among the leading universities in the country. As researchers Steven T. Sonka and David L. Chicoine have observed, "Land grants were early innovators creating structural capabilities to transfer research results to the market."

The great state universities were molded and are influenced to this day by entrepreneurial early presidents such as Daniel Coit Gilman of the University of California–Berkeley (and later of Johns Hopkins), John Bascom of the University of Wisconsin, and Henry Tappan of the University of Michigan. They were entrepreneurial leaders who saw their institutions as a bridge for the citizenry who sought education but were often not prepared for the rigor of life in a research environment. And so they did much to build the high school system to ensure that students entered universities ready to undertake the challenge of curricula in engineering, agriculture, and the emerging technologies.

The Morrill Act firmly tied the American university to the

American economy. But in the postbellum period, five entrepreneurs established universities that changed the game. These founders understood how important technology had been in creating their own fortunes and could see how critical research would be to the continued growth of the American economy.

When Ezra Cornell, founder of Western Union, created Cornell University in 1865, he expressly embraced the implications of the Morrill Act's intent to stimulate higher education in "practical subjects," as opposed to the heavy emphasis on the classics that characterized other private colleges. That decision would influence other private universities and signaled the coming of a new institution, the modern research university. (Cornell itself pioneered a public/private model. This private Ivy League university is home to New York State's land-grant college of agriculture.)

Johns Hopkins, who had made his fortune in shipping and by financing the Baltimore and Ohio, the nation's first railroad, had no grand vision of creating a new form of institution. But, by hiring Daniel Coit Gilman away from the University of California, he brought to Baltimore perhaps the most influential university president in American history.

Gilman saw the German universities and research institutes as his model. He sought to promote advanced research and scholarship and create an environment that "actively encouraged original investigations by its faculty." Gilman actively recruited the best scholars and offered them freedom from many of the routine teaching requirements of other universities. In fact, during its first fifteen years, graduate students outnumbered undergraduates at Johns Hopkins!

Progress and the use of knowledge for the betterment of society were now indelibly part of the core of a university's purpose.

The third entrepreneurial founder was John D. Rockefeller,

who created two new models of higher education. The first was the University of Chicago in 1890. Like Gilman at Hopkins a generation before him, the University of Chicago's first president, William Rainey Harper, recruited the best faculty, often paying them twice what they were receiving elsewhere. But Rockefeller, who twenty-one years later would found the Rockefeller Institute for Medical Research (now Rockefeller University), exerted a very creative and influential hand in the early years of the University of Chicago. He intended the school, which he would later call the best investment of his life, to be a locus of premier research, one that would "have a pervasive influence" in improving society.

Rockefeller, by now an experienced philanthropist, said:

> Following the principle of trying to abolish evils by destroying them at their source, we felt that to aid colleges and universities, whose graduates would spread their culture far and wide, was the surest way to fight ignorance and promote the growth of *useful knowledge*.

Leland Stanford, the fourth entrepreneurial founder, dreamed of a university that would excel at "practical education." As a prosperous businessman—he built the Central Pacific railroad—he observed that college education was not preparing young people for success: "Of all the young men who come to me with letters of introduction from friends in the East, the most helpless are college young men." In 1891, he set out to create an institution that in his words would "qualify students for personal success and direct usefulness in life."

One last entrepreneur who created a university (actually,

like Rockefeller, two) was George Eastman. Like the others, Eastman was not a college graduate. Yet he clearly saw the link between America's future and university education, particularly in
engineering.

While Eastman is remembered for creating the University of
Rochester and turning it into a very strong research model, few
know he is also responsible for saving the Massachusetts Institute of
Technology from closing. While Eastman's gift was unknown until
his death in 1932, he provided the funds to move MIT to its current
location in Cambridge and to erect its grand neoclassical main
building.

These men helped create a new type of university, one based on
providing both a practical education and excellent research designed to help sustain the new nation. The entrepreneurial creators
of these institutions made sure that the university became a preeminent player in the nation's economy.

But our colleges and universities are no longer as entrepreneurial as they once were. They have become kludged up and bogged
down by both bureaucracy and, as we shall see, a loss of direction.
Ironically, these problems stem from internal cultural forces that
seem dead set against the practical and the entrepreneurial, the twin
pillars upon which universities were created in the first place.

We can point to at least four specific areas in which it is easy to
see that our universities have lost their way: (1) the decline of science and engineering as fields of importance; (2) the creation of
studies that yield uneducated "educated" graduates, many of whom
have absorbed an antibusiness perspective as part of the university
experience; (3) attempts to reinvent the university into a corporate
organism that makes money on its discoveries; and (4) a bloated bureaucracy and cost structure.

## The Diminished Role of Science and Engineering

While the number of students majoring in science and engineering has held steady, market demand has been growing at nearly twice the rate of the production of math and science majors. So we are actually falling behind. And the numbers look worse when we only consider native-born Americans.

The number of native-born students majoring in math and science has been falling. Our overall production of science and engineering majors has been constant only because of the admission of foreign nationals, a predominant number of whom seek American university experience in just these disciplines.

The result? The nation is facing a severe shortage of engineers and people trained at the Ph.D. level in technology. The National Science Board (NSB) of the National Science Foundation could not have been grimmer in its 2004 assessment of what this means:

> If the trends . . . continue . . . three things will happen. The number of jobs in the U.S. economy that require sciences and engineering training will grow; the number of U.S. citizens prepared for those jobs will, at best, be level; and the availability of people from other countries who have science and engineering training [to fill the gap] will decline, either because of limits to entry imposed by U.S. national security restrictions or because of intense global competition for people with these skills. Even if action is taken today to change these trends, the reversal is 10 to 20 years away.

The problem the NSB sees is compounded by the importance of engineering graduates to the entrepreneurial ecosystem. Nearly

85 percent of all the high-growth businesses created in the United States in the last twenty years have been established by people with a college degree. Of these university-educated founders, engineering was the predominant major. And the real shortage the nation faces with its supply of engineers may actually be worse than it appears, because the supply of practicing engineers is getting older. Within the next ten years, it has been estimated that as many as 40 percent of them will retire.

## Courses That Are Not Courses

As we discussed earlier, American society and the American economy have undergone a deep transformation. We are now able to discern an entrepreneurial ecosystem that requires different knowledge and skills than the models that preceded it. Universities are the key institutions in responding to this transformation, since they bear both a responsibility to society and a responsibility to individual students to prepare them with a general foundation of learning, intellectual curiosity, and critical thinking abilities—in short, the tools that will enable them to adapt and succeed in an entrepreneurial economy.

Many contemporary universities have not recognized these profound economic and societal changes and thus have done their students a disservice by failing to give them an education relevant to those changes. How can our universities be failing to educate the entrepreneurs of tomorrow (and that means everyone)?

One common—though unacceptable—answer is that universities are merely responding to the market. If a high percentage of students want training for specific jobs, many of which have little to do with what the economy will need and reward in the future, then the universities have no choice but to supply it. Competition for students leaves no other alternative.

A casual inventory of available majors in colleges and universities speaks loudly to how what is essentially vocational training has displaced a sound general education, which used to be the common denominator among truly educated people. Students can major in game design, alternative medicine, packaging, corporate training, music therapy, economic crime (with a minor, seriously, in corporate fraud detection), teacher licensure (that includes whole courses in evaluating textbooks), leadership, sports and leisure studies, recording arts technology, athletic training, and marine animal rescue.

And there is no shortage of takers. For example, the number of students majoring in parks, recreation, leisure, and fitness studies has grown by 1,222 percent in the last thirty years! A federal study in 2004 found that most undergraduate students were enrolled in "career-oriented" majors, as opposed to academic majors.

In a related trend, students are taking courses—often a concentration of them—in areas that would never have been recognized by the legendary educators we discussed earlier. To cite just one example, at Goucher College, a respected liberal arts college in Maryland, students can minor in "peace studies," described by the university as:

Based on an understanding that differences enrich our lives and that conflicts provide opportunities for growth, peace studies proposes ways of being in the world that incorporate the skills of listening and dialogue, mediation and negotiation, ideas of rights balanced with responsibilities, questions of justice, and philosophies of non-violence. As the 21st century finds us living in a world where violence has become banal, where subliminal, virtual, or actual violence bombards us all in every walk of life, where armed political and economic conflicts divide the world again into fiefdoms of ethnicity or privilege, so, too, alternatives exist by which we can live.

Couple these "innovations" with the emergence of psychology as the second most common major and you have a picture of today's universities reflecting a world in which educated people are to be content with lives revolving around very specific work, or maintaining what might be thought of as societal narcissism, in which we focus on our feelings and our individual health.

Such a turn in college curriculum has the effect of denying students what to many people is the most important single skill—namely, critical thinking—that higher education is supposed to develop. One outcome, and a worrisome one, is that some students default to the "correct" opinion, one that is decidedly hostile toward American corporations. This attitude readily finds itself into the course material.

While our corporations are not perfect, and many have engaged in reprehensible behavior in the past (e.g., General Electric dumping toxins into the Hudson River) and in the near present (e.g., Enron, Tyco, and WorldCom), the American corporation is the only source of economic wealth in our society. And, while among the millions of U.S. corporations some will engage in illegal and unethical conduct, the vast majority operate as honorable institutions attempting to produce the goods and services that consumers seek at the lowest possible price.

There is little doubt, however, that university faculties have assumed a general hostility toward corporations and what they represent. "In [university-based politically correct thought] capitalism is a particular object of loathing," Michael Novak has observed. Poll data demonstrate that such antibusiness bias has in fact seeped into students' psyches. The result is that policy solutions proposed in nearly all disciplines look to government to regulate the market more closely. In short, prejudice against business is assumed.

Just take a look at how Wal-Mart is viewed on college campuses. It is seen as about the worst thing that ever happened to American life. It is despised for its offshore supply chains that are said to exploit native workers; for its destruction of small-town merchants; for its abusive conduct toward its employees, which includes failing to provide health insurance; and for its antiunion posture. It is not uncommon to see students attempting to boycott the local Wal-Mart. I have talked with innumerable academics who believe that to patronize the company is morally reprehensive.

Yet seldom do you hear of the positive implications of Sam Walton's vision. Walton foresaw that making routine household items—everything from dishwashing detergent to lawn mowers—affordable for lower income families was a way to make customers' lives better! Wal-Mart stores have inarguably improved life for lower-income families by significantly lowering their cost of living.

The objective of every business is to make products that people need and to compete for their attention by continuously improving those products and lowering prices. But this reality is either not appreciated or expressly overlooked by campus populations that see corporate achievement as intrinsically wrong.

Worse, the essence of what many academics believe and teach is that the only acceptable counterweight for business is a larger and larger government producing an ever-expanding set of rules and regulations to check the power of corporations. This position appears to overlook the obvious. Without the efforts of corporations and the people who work in them, we would not have the wealth as a society to afford to create and sustain our universities. And yet universities are seemingly going out of the way to hinder the ability of America to succeed economically in the future.

Providing students solely with specific skills, such as learning how to be a corporate fraud detector, will make it very hard for them to adjust when the economy evolves, as it inevitably will. And promoting ideology—business is inherently evil—over dispassionate critical reasoning skills is just silly. We need to be teaching our students how to think more clearly, not inculcating them with ideology or telling them there are certain roads of intellectual inquiry they should not pursue.

The incident at Harvard in early 2005 involving former university president Lawrence H. Summers serves as a case in point. Summers, speaking at a National Bureau of Economic Research Conference on Diversifying the Science & Engineering Workforce, suggested in passing that perhaps innate or biological differences in the sexes might explain why fewer women succeed in science and math careers. It is an interesting suggestion, and you would have thought that someone at a great university such as Harvard would have been interested in finding out if it were true.

Instead, Summers was branded as a misogynist—and worse—and there were calls for his resignation, which were eventually heeded. Unfortunately, the Summers episode is far too typical. Increasingly, universities are intolerant of the basic discussions that promote research—or could. In many areas, academic "research" is simply consistent with what is promoted by government agencies and foundations that provide funding or with what is believed by the consensus.

Consensus positions don't fall; paradigm shifts don't happen; people don't think differently in a world where intellectual, cultural, or political elites know the answer before the question is asked or make it almost impossible to ask the question in the first place. We must give disturbing ideas or troublesome counterexamples time to be resolved or to tip over the whole consensus.

We need to be ever watchful of the opportunity presented when the facts don't fit. It requires an open mind, honest dialogue among a group of trusted colleagues, and a supportive environment that rewards and is comfortable with new thoughts and the risky implications they present for the real world. That seems to be happening less and less, which is both extremely troubling and runs counter to why universities were initially founded.

In 1872, John Henry Cardinal Newman wrote that a true university is "a place where inquiry is pushed forward, and discoveries verified and perfected, and rashness rendered innocuous, and error exposed, by the collision of mind with mind, and knowledge with knowledge." Testing boundaries, asking questions, and challenging assumptions is in some sense what we could call knowledge entrepreneurship, the imperative we expect from universities and those who participate in entrepreneurial capitalism.

For universities to shift away from a broad, basic liberal education that includes grounding in mathematics and science threatens the production of the human talent needed to sustain the entrepreneurial ecosystem. Ultimately, it will result in the production of young adults incapable of being creative and innovative contributors to society.

Worse, they may not be equipped for the changes they will face in their careers. Since American workers change jobs (and sometimes careers) many times before they retire, critical thinking skills are an invaluable asset. Narrow vocationalism simply does not prepare our students to deal with the next opportunity nearly as well as a liberal education that allows them to realize the full range of their potentialities.

Higher education should graduate intellectually curious students prepared to make innovative contributions to society and the economy. That will be the only way to succeed in the entrepreneurial economy ahead.

## High Overhead

The university is also at risk of failing to play its central role in the entrepreneurial ecosystem because of the enormous expansion of its bureaucracy and overhead expenses. The problem here is multifold.

For every dollar a company or the government wants to spend on research, a university typically now demands another 70 cents to fund central operations (overhead)—that is, to subsidize the faculties who frequently protest the presence of science and engineering that might be used for commercial gain. As the cost of conducting research at universities has continued to rise, increasing amounts of corporate-sponsored research are moving overseas to foreign universities, which continue to make remarkable academic strides.

And then, as every parent knows too well, there is the matter of tuition. For the last twenty years, college tuition costs have risen faster than the consumer price index. From 1982 to 2002, tuition rose 6.12 percent a year on average while the cost of living for all other goods and services rose 3.3 percent (see graph).

One response has been the rise in for-profit colleges, where a credit hour is significantly less expensive. The University of Phoenix, a for-profit corporation, prices its credit hours at $350, while Georgetown charges $1,319. Some of Phoenix's newer competitors charge only $150 per credit hour.

This could explain why for-profit universities continue to gain market share. Nationally, enrollment in these commercial institu-

## Tuition and Inflation Growth

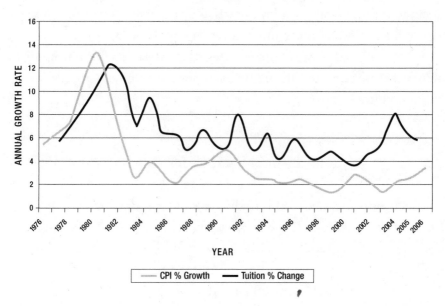

YEAR

CPI % Growth      Tuition % Change

tions rose 147 percent from 1995 to 2002 to almost 600,000 students.

Whereas colleges and universities once might have defended themselves by pointing to the consistently distinct and high-quality product they produce, the argument is harder and harder to advance when majors such as marine mammal rescue and teacher credentialing become more and more common. At some point, consumers always take a hard look at what they get for their money.

What is responsible for the growth of university costs? We know it is not instructional expenses. At many schools over the last twenty years, costs for things such as student services and institution support rose at faster rates than costs for instruction. With this increased spending on noninstructional activities came more nonfaculty staff. As economist Richard Vedder has shown, since 1976 the faculty/student ratio has risen only slightly, while the number of "other professional" staff skyrocketed by 92 perecnt. This category includes administrators, administrative assistants to administrators, counselors, and technical and maintenance positions.

Given that the great universities were founded by entrepreneurs, it is nothing but ironic that the American university has become so bureaucratic.

## The Technology Transfer Mess

Despite bureaucracies and high costs, universities create huge amounts of new knowledge. Unfortunately, they have looked upon their research activities recently as a way to become rich, by selling the intellectual property produced, instead of—as historically had been done—making it available for free as a public good.

The result: a major case of greed and bureaucracy rolled into one. Schools want to get paid enormous sums for what is discovered on campus, yet they have invented a huge bureaucracy that slows the process tremendously, compounding the need for more income (to support the bureaucracy).

Companies such as Hewlett Packard, IBM, and Dow Chemical that once sponsored a great deal of basic research and development at universities, in their quest for new ideas, are now funding foreign universities because their research processes are much more efficient. Let's examine how and why over the last twenty-five years many universities have fashioned themselves into for-profit laboratory companies.

The transformation was made possible by the passage of the Bayh-Dole Act, which gave the property rights in discoveries stemming from university research funded by the federal government to the university where the research took place. Like so many acts of Congress, the Bayh-Dole Act has had unintended consequences, both positive and negative. We have touched on the positives already. (See Chapter 3 for a discussion of the new products and innovations that have flowed directly out of university research.) But it is worth spending some time on the negative consequences as well.

As a result of the Bayh-Dole Act, research—which universities had always seen as an expense, as a cost of doing business—is now viewed as an activity expected to make money for the university. An entire bureaucracy—typically called offices of technology transfer—has sprung up to make sure this happens. Considered to be revenue centers, these offices are tasked implicitly or explicitly with generating specific targeted amounts of revenue for the university.

And yet, counterintuitively, universities make it difficult for that to occur. For example, if a company provides funding for a certain line of research and a breakthrough is made, the university is likely to step forward and assert its rights to patent the invention. Taking the first step in what in many cases is a long chain of bureaucratic processes, this slows the progress of the new invention to the market.

Look at the situation from the perspective of a company that supports the research. The company not only pays for research, but if that research is successful, it often must pay again (to buy the patent), in addition to the implicit time cost of university bureaucratic delay. The company must also face the situation that if it does not offer what the university considers to be a sufficient amount, the university could sell the intellectual property to a competitor.

Seldom does a week go by that I don't hear from a professor who is certain he has a significant discovery. He holds patents on it, knows there are substantial commercial applications, and starts down the route of taking his idea to market only to have the university step in, naively establishing high expectations for the value of the discovery or deciding to pursue a commercial relationship with the wrong partner. Companies that "buy" or support research find the growing complexity and uncertainty of dealing with American universities increasingly unattractive, and many are choosing to sponsor research in foreign universities.

The proliferation of offices of technology transfer that can be found on at least three hundred fifty campuses, compared with the very small number of discovery-producing universities, suggests that many schools have unrealistic perceptions of the economic importance of their faculties' research. If you divide the aggregate revenues resulting from university research by the number of technology transfer offices, you find that each university on average is receiving just $3 million annually, a small amount given the tens of billions of research dollars universities receive every year.

## There Is Some Hope

There are isolated examples of extraordinarily entrepreneurial behavior on campus. More important, there are schools that have incorporated entrepreneurial activity as a theme of instruction.

Cornell and Iowa State serve as cases in point. They not only support entrepreneurial work among their faculty but also transmit these values to their students. In each case, they have developed an entrepreneurial perspective on curriculum that involves exposing students at all levels to the idea that they may create a business during their career. This message to students is not only should they be prepared to do so, but the university will be helpful in providing research as well as support to them as students or as alumni. Faculty members know that the institution is not simply tolerant of entrepreneurial faculty members, but actually supportive and encouraging. In both schools, entrepreneurship is an institutional goal encouraged by the president.

The approach taken by Cornell and Iowa State is being copied by eight other universities under a program sponsored by the Kauffman Foundation. These institutions (Florida International University, Howard University, the University of Illinois at Urbana-Champaign, the University of North Carolina, the University of Rochester, the University of Texas at El Paso, Washington University in St. Louis, and Wake Forest University) have made a wide array of courses on entrepreneurship available to all students regardless of their major.

Three reasons underlie this policy. First, campus business schools pay little attention to the study of business formation. Second, typical business faculties are traditionally reluctant to create courses for nonbusiness students. Most business schools look at themselves as studying an encapsulated set of insights presumed to be of little interest to students not enrolled in the business curriculum. Even worse is an implicit assumption that students who are not dedicated to studying business are not central to the teaching mission of the business school.

But, by far, the third reason is the most powerful. These eight schools anticipate the experiences their graduates will have. They know their alumni will create new businesses, so it is important for the university to prepare them for this aspect of their lives. These universities have not created new majors in entrepreneurship but have decided that the students, regardless of their major, should understand what entrepreneurs do.

Happily, there is evidence that these cross-campus programs are spreading. These programs that exist outside of the business school treat entrepreneurship much as they used to teach subjects as part of a liberal education; that is, exposure to the theory and history of entrepreneurship prepares students for the possibility that they might be involved in an entrepreneurial activity during their lives.

In addition, some universities are rethinking their approach to technology transfer. For example, the dean of the engineering school at Carnegie Mellon University, Pradeep Khosla, has adopted a new philosophy and approach. He has created a new research collaborative called CyLab, whose mission is to build information infrastructure that is secure and sustainable in all circumstances, even if attacked.

But instead of having professors coming up with discoveries that the university then tries to sell to the highest bidder, the lab starts from a different perspective. It has two guiding philosophies: (1) a university's job is to maximize research funding, not licensing income and (2) the university's discoveries should be available to a wide array of users who support a research "commons" with general funding.

The lab receives federal research dollars, of course, but also funding from as many as fifty companies that each provides $500,000 annually. In exchange, every firm has a nonexclusive, royalty-free right to use any research discovery coming from CyLab. In the CyLab model there is no need for a bureaucracy to manage technology transfer. That makes the corporate participants happy, as does the fact that they get to leverage their investment. They put up $500,000, but they get the benefit of $25 million worth of research—plus whatever the federal government provides. And as more firms join, the leverage expands.

In a different model, a consortium of universities—the University of California-Berkeley, Stanford University, the University of Wisconsin, Washington University, and the University of North

Carolina—working with the Kauffman Foundation has developed a similar way of making their innovation process more efficient. Called iBridge, the consortium is creating a common market for technologies developed by each school.

The new entity, which in a sense is like a high-tech eBay, provides an efficient market for developed technologies. Great efficiency gains are expected as universities use iBridge's common contract and post their offerings on an automated marketplace. iBridge is seen as potentially a first step in ultimately eliminating individual technology transfer offices, especially in smaller universities with very little deal flow.

There are other hopeful signs. A number of universities are innovating around the very process of how education is conducted and how universities might be reassembled to become more entrepreneurial. Stanford, for example, has recently initiated a new approach to research and teaching engineering and the life sciences. Called Bio-X, the approach reflects the concerted thinking of both entrepreneurs and industrial designers engaged to think about how to make a teaching/learning environment to foster entrepreneurial activity that could result in viable commercial applications.

David Kelly, a professor at Stanford and founder of IDEO, a world-famous industrial design firm, worked on the curriculum as well as the plan for the physical space. James Clark, a successful entrepreneur who founded, among other companies, Netscape and Healtheon, donated the cost of a new building that symbolically has been built between the engineering and medical schools.

It is, of course, the curriculum that is important. Bio-X purposively brings students together from different backgrounds with a view that new knowledge will be conceived at the intersection of disciplines. The university has changed its curriculum accordingly. For example, the medical school has decided that any newly created tenured faculty position must be interdisciplinary in nature. The number of faculty in traditional departments, therefore, is frozen.

A second change is the decision to require five years to obtain a medical degree at Stanford, instead of the traditional four, to incorporate all the new research requirements that are part of the degree. This change is a declaration that Stanford will become the first medical school where students self-select because they want to pursue careers in research or, at the very least, have a research component as part of their medical education.

Another example is the move by the University of Wisconsin to merge the medical school with its public health program to create the School of Medicine and Public Health. This is the first such integration in the country.

The goal, according to former UW Medical School dean Philip Farrell, is to shift "from health care that responds to individual illness and injury to a more balanced strategy of prevention efforts aimed at promoting health in large groups of people." The new strategy, in an interdisciplinary manner, will bring together faculty from population health sciences, family medicine, biostatistics, medical informatics, nutritional sciences, social work, nursing, pharmacy, veterinary medicine, and public affairs. By combining teaching, research, and service, the integrated program will not only generate an impact on people's health but also produce a competitive advantage for the university for federal research dollars and private donations.

Pursuing a new combination of existing elements, striving for social impact, working to distinguish itself from its competitors— these are all examples of a university acting entrepreneurially. An even larger effort to explicitly change the entire course of a university is underway at Arizona State, where under the leadership of

President Michael Crow, ASU has declared itself the new American university.

Faced with enormous demand (state officials believe ASU will have to double its current enrollment of 45,000 by 2020), Crow is reshaping the school to prepare students for the future. For example, the new School of Economics and the Environment will combine several of the traditional disciplines around a new core of courses designed to create a fresh perspective on environmental issues. Crow sees such "recombinant disciplines" as critical to creating an entrepreneurial university, one that efficiently produces new knowledge over a wider range of human interests. He envisions several of these new schools at ASU.

Dr. Crow is acting on what many in universities know, namely, that the division of knowledge into traditional departments and schools actually impedes progress. By recombining various disciplines, ASU is developing an entirely new university from within, one preparing students for a new economic order.

The steps being undertaken at Stanford, ASU, and the University of Wisconsin are promising. Unfortunately, those schools are the exception.

## What Needs to Be Done

Universities, founded as entrepreneurial institutions that would help create the new, no longer are. Bureaucracy has set in. Universities have forgotten or, worse, repudiated the entrepreneurial imperative that created the fortunes that allowed their benefactors to start them in the first place.

Things need to change. How?

When you are trying to change any institution, be it a company, foundation, church, or, in this case, a university, the wise manager places a new vision before the organization. You move toward the new. You don't fight or quarrel with the past.

Let's use an example. Suppose Lawrence Summers, the deposed president of Harvard, set out to reinvigorate Harvard as he was hired to do. And suppose he had said, "We have a huge capital endowment, somewhere on the order of $25 billion." (Universities seldom use this capital; they merely spend the interest.)

Now suppose he said to the faculty and the world: "The greatest problem humanity faces is poverty in Africa, and Harvard is going to do something about it. We're going to take $2 billion of our endowment—less than 10 percent of the total—and create a university in the sub-Sahara. I will ask the faculty to spend every sixth year teaching there, and I will be spending every sixth year there as well."

This move would have been so galvanizing that Summers would have had enormous power over the faculty—moral power. He then could have begun to reshape the university toward the future that is necessary if Harvard is to remain a preeminent university. He could have required faculty in various interdisciplinary centers to produce work of the same intellectual rigor required of the traditional disciplines operating as formal departments—one of his initial goals. And, in no time at all, an excited alumni base would likely have more than replaced the $2 billion. It would have been an entrepreneurial solution to how you change a set-in-its-ways bureaucratic institution.

This kind of radical approach is possible. If Stanford can insist that every new M.D. is going to be a scientist and ASU can establish entirely new schools of cross-disciplinary studies such as economics and the environment, change is possible. But notice what was a central part of both of those change initiatives: The people running these institutions saw themselves as partners in the advancement of American democratic capitalism as a means of improving human welfare. That is in stark contrast to what is occurring in many other institutions.

Changing universities will be difficult. They are institutions beset by two disabilities. The first is huge bureaucracy.

Second, it is difficult to reform an institution where the key human capital, the faculty, has gathered power unto itself over the years. Thanks to tenure, bizarre anti-intellectual episodes like the one Summers went through at Harvard are possible. Not only was he unable to initiate his reforms, his faculty forced him to resign, instead of responding to a needed strategic adjustment of mission.

To shape an institution, the executive must have the power to require continuous performance in the classroom and laboratory. I am a devout believer in academic freedom. But academic freedom relates to what is taught in the classroom. Professors *should* be protected to teach things that are not conventional wisdom. They must also have the freedom to investigate and research, to "sift and winnow" as they see fit. But they should not have veto power over the course the institution takes. This was never the intent when universities were established; nor is it in the tradition of tenure and free speech.

## The Possibilities

Universities create ideas—intellectual property—that fuel the continued development and growth of the economy. But they could do so much more. They could also transmit the values that would help students understand how important their role is in building wealth in society.

Universities should prepare students for what lies ahead. Well over half of all university graduates will start a business during the course of their lives. Universities must convey the commonness of this experience and prepare students for the moment when it will happen.

I chose that wording carefully. I am not saying that universities should be training grounds for twenty-year-old entrepreneurs. Not only do most people who are twenty lack the necessary experience for starting a business, but they may not have an idea for creating one.

Universities do need to expose students to the likelihood that they might want to start a business or convert an idea into a commercial organization at some point in their lives. Finally, every student should know that entrepreneurs play a central role in the economic welfare of society. Perhaps the easiest way to make that happen is to eliminate everything in the university environment that is standing in the way. Here are some suggestions:

- Colleges should get out of the business of teaching specific skills such as fraud detection. Let's return to the liberal arts and sciences that provide students with insights and skills that permit them constantly to adapt to the challenges and opportunities of life.
- We should close schools of education that obviously are not working. Math teachers should be trained as math majors! Science teachers should be trained in the sciences. You don't need to be an education major to teach.
- I am not proposing more entrepreneurship courses per se, but they are important and should be available to every undergraduate.

• Universities should be delivering content that will allow entrepreneurship to flourish, which means an increased emphasis on science and math.

## The Problem with Business Schools

Our business schools have the chance to take the lead in shaping the future. But they will need to change radically to do so.

Our economy is changing; the very nature of capitalism is changing. Not only have most business schools been slow to adjust, but many are moving in the wrong direction. In fact, it might be said that the contemporary business school is an institution that is not working.

The evidence is everywhere. Business schools face competition from every quarter: newly formed international schools, American undergraduate institutions, and online universities. In response, it seems, the traditional business schools are expanding their curriculum, and as a result, diluting their focus. New courses are springing up involving "Yoga and Business." I suppose "Pilates and Supply Chain Management" is just around the corner. It is not surprising that a Stanford study shows the rate of return to students on MBA training is positive for only a handful of schools.

Some will suggest that great business schools have nothing to fear. Look at their dedicated endowments, they'll say. Look at the support they enjoy in the highest circles of business leadership, both domestically and abroad. Why should we fix something that is not broken?

I would suggest that to ask this question reflects the problem. You either adapt or become irrelevant. Boeing, which made what we would refer to today as prop planes, was the market leader in the 1950s. But instead of saying, "If it ain't broke, don't fix it," it made a

THE ENTREPRENEURIAL IMPERATIVE

bet-the-company decision on producing planes powered by jet engines. If it hadn't, it would have become another New York Central Railroad. Today, Boeing is making another bet-the-company play with its Dreamliner model.

Business schools must also change radically. The canon of what they teach is thin. The theory of business, what it does and its role in society, is impossibly undeveloped. Business is not seen as a calling. In short, despite the fact that everything looks good on the outside, the business school core is hollow because it has missed the turn—the profound metamorphosis of the American economy.

We have entered an era of entrepreneurial capitalism. That is now the heart of our economy, but it is not at the heart of what is being taught at our business schools. In fact, what is being taught is a far cry from Joseph Wharton's vision when he funded the first business school. Wharton pictured a school that would prepare students for the "profession of business." They would graduate as well-rounded managers who would serve a dynamic economy. His gift to the University of Pennsylvania was, as we have seen, consistent with other philanthropic entrepreneurs who saw the role of higher education as supporting and advancing the continuous development of democratic capitalism.

Wharton's vision, however, underwent radical change decades ago when graduate business training was reconceived as an exercise in quantitative thinking. The MBA was deprofessionalized and made into a kind of financial engineering degree. The qualitative view of business as an integral part of the saga of an ever-evolving America was abandoned, dismissed as well-meaning but misguided by academics who sought to make business schools home to scientific methods and language.

This occurred in the 1950s. This view, as we saw earlier, was helped along by the times. American business benefited enormously from the expansion of the military demands of the Cold War. With the government as the ultimate customer, most of America's largest companies became accustomed to bureaucratic ways. Government cost-plus contracting and bureaucratic purchasing procedures encouraged a stable economy and a bureaucratic mindset. Accountants had a chance of becoming CEOs!

It was this world that the modern business school sought to serve and unfortunately continues to serve. A professor at one of the nation's most respected business schools recently wrote me that "MBA programs train students for bureaucracy. This reflects the fact that too many schools define their 'customers' as the corporate recruiters from large firms."

Indeed, business schools are training students for old-style American corporations, not American business as it has evolved. Our entrepreneurial economy has become the predominant model for growth and development worldwide. But some of the last people in the world to "get it" have been the faculties in our nation's business schools. Thus, the question becomes, How does the American business school reinvent itself—or should I say re-reinvent itself—so that it's in tune with our entrepreneurial economy?

As we have seen, the answer is more complicated than simply adding more courses on entrepreneurship. While courses and programs in entrepreneurship are helpful, they're not sufficient. I believe a more comprehensive approach guided by five key principles is called for.

## Creating the New B School

*First, the business school curriculum must focus on where our economy is headed, not where it used to be.* That means economics must be the central focus of this new curriculum. Economics, after all, is the only discipline designed to understand relationships between markets, individual motives, the movement of capital, and the importance of government policy.

If economics had been at the core of business school education in recent years, undoubtedly the move into the new era of entrepreneurial capitalism would be understood more fully. The changing nature of competition and the recomposition of firms over the last twenty years would have suggested a new market environment.

*Second, business schools must take a different view of strategy.* Strategy must be informed first and foremost by an appreciation of technology. Technological change is the single most important force moving our economy, yet, reading business strategists, technology almost seems incidental to the issues the manager confronts today!

Furthermore, the instruction of strategy needs more strongly to acknowledge that the ability to adapt is key. Unbelievably, 84 percent of Inc. 500 entrepreneurs report the business they started is substantially different in product offering and customer base than the firm they are running today.

*Third, risk assessment must be taught.* Business students must be taught the core skill of capitalism: how to assess and manage risk. To my mind, too much emphasis is placed on financial analysis and not enough on risk analysis. The study of financial ploys and accounting innovations is important. But such steps never create wealth. They may release, realign, redeploy, or accelerate the creation of wealth, but they cannot create it.

Taking calculated risks is how new ways of making wealth and expanding social welfare come about. No business student should be graduated without an understanding of risk.

*Fourth, we need better and more relevant research.* We need empirically based insights into business, especially when it comes to entre-preneurship. Our current knowledge about entrepreneurship is roughly equivalent to what we knew about medicine a hundred years ago. Unfortunately, most business schools are not set up to provide the big research thrust we need. This must change if we are truly to understand and optimize the entrepreneurial process.

*Fifth, the case method must be examined, especially in teaching entre-preneurship.* Case studies are valuable learning tools. They can bring learning to life by having students analyze real-world situations and think on their own. But these tools have to be used properly, and they have to be part of a larger educational toolkit.

I have visited schools where the introductory thirteen-week twice-weekly course in entrepreneurship is "taught" by twenty-six successful alumni entrepreneurs who tell their life's stories. While often inspirational, I wonder how much rigorous analysis and syn-thesis is going on here.

Students should not have to synthesize the basic rules and prin-ciples of the field. Rather, the job of the researchers and teachers is to study the field, determine what is generally true, then impart that knowledge and encourage students to see how it might be applied. Case method is one way to do that, but so is the Socratic method and any other method that ingenious educators can come up with.

Finally, one of the best ways for students to learn from business cases is actually to experience them via real-world internships—and more of these internships need to be entrepreneurially ori-ented—with entrepreneurial companies, the venture arms of large companies, or within venture capital firms.

The regeneration of our business schools should mirror the on-going rebirth of American capitalism. Every time an entrepreneur takes the risky course of starting a business or resetting the course of an existing institution, both capitalism and democracy are renewed. No business or civic endeavor is more important. Business schools should help make that effort easier. After all, that is what people like Joseph Wharton intended.

## Summing Up How Universities Can Help the Entrepreneurial Imperative

For entrepreneurial capitalism to succeed, universities must become the most entrepreneurial of institutions. Many, however, continue to perform suboptimally, hampered by enormously bureaucratic cultures and a mindset almost universally opposed to capitalism.

This cannot continue. Our economic growth depends more and more on the success of our research universities. Constant innovation and the entropic expansion of knowledge place enormous demands on universities, and only an entrepreneurial response will suffice.

Implicit in making the university an entrepreneurial institution is an understanding that insights into the future will be hastened by encouraging disciplines to broaden their approach to creating knowledge. Indeed, it may be time for individual departments within the university to be declared obsolete and done away with. New ones may need to be created, but the departmentalization of knowledge itself should be examined.

Of course, many will resist such a move because of their loyalty and sense of security within the discipline. Many tenured faculty members scoff and successfully resist the calls of presidents to reinvent the university along different lines with different incentives. Almost by definition they will not be the entrepreneurial intellectuals who will push disciplines into the future.

One free market solution is to have universities compete for federal funds. Competition will keep internal bureaucracies from overwhelming universities entirely. As in business, bureaucracy emerges as the challenge to continued innovation. This is not unexpected. Bureaucracy finds all entrepreneurial behavior abhorrent. Bureaucracy is the enemy of innovation, the arterial plaque in an economy.

Competition is the key to making our universities innovate and act entrepreneurially. If a college or university realizes it cannot compete in a world where a comprehensive liberal arts education is the basis of all learning, the market should push it out of business.

Universities, of all the institutions of the entrepreneurial ecosystem, are the ones most at risk. They have, with some exceptions, developed a contemporary culture antithetical to entrepreneurial activity.

But, even more important, the students they produce are not as ready as they once were to be contributing members of an increasingly entrepreneurial society. Unless this changes, our nation's economic future is in peril.

★

# 7

# EXPORTING ENTREPRENEURSHIP

*A plan for worldwide peace and prosperity*

SINCE THE END OF THE COLD WAR, the hope has been that every nation will soon be free. Yet we in the so-called free world are not entirely sure how to propagate freedom—how best to nourish it in other lands. Much of our policy is still grounded in rather simplistic modes of thinking shaped by the Cold War era: if we encourage democracy and give direct aid to those who head down that path, somehow representative governments will naturally flourish.

But this approach has often yielded disappointing results. Many economies in Latin America, Eastern Europe, and elsewhere are stagnant or backsliding, and most of the world's poorest economies show few signs of new life.

Does that mean our approach is wrong? No. But it needs to be supplemented. Going forward, the American economic model should not be abandoned, as some development economists advocate, but improved. The current template is incomplete. In particular, it fails to reproduce a vital element of the U.S. economy: support for entrepreneurship.

The approach we now take focuses on macroeconomic issues such as finance and trade, along with general institution building. Nations are urged to create good banking systems, reasonable interest and exchange rates, and stable tax structures. They are expected to privatize, deregulate, and invest in infrastructure and basic education.

Entrepreneurship, meanwhile, is considered only as an afterthought and in a piecemeal fashion. Some policy makers, for instance, have suggested that venture capital firms should be added to the list of financial institutions that developing countries ought to have. But venture capital will do no good without ventures to support. Real opportunities arise only when a nation is the initiator: a breeder of new firms based on new ideas that add unique value.

Entrepreneurship is what enables American-style capitalism to be generative and self-renewing. The problem confronting policy makers is to model the entrepreneurial dimension of the U.S. economy in a way that is comprehensive enough to capture all the important dynamics and is also transferable to other economies. This chapter contains just such a plan.

## How to Spread Entrepreneurship Around the World

A quick reprise will set the stage for how we can export entrepreneurship around the world. As we have seen, the American entrepreneurial system involves four institutions within our economy. The first sector is inhabited by new firms. The people who start them need not be scientists or inventors of new products themselves. Henry Ford did not create the automobile and Michael Dell did not invent any computer technology. Both built their firms largely around production and marketing ideas, freely borrowing from existing concepts.

Ford's moving assembly line was inspired by production at meat-packing plants. Dell lowered the cost of PCs by building them to order rather than carrying inventory and by selling directly so as to eliminate the dealer. Both ideas had been used by other industries.

Business mythology portrays new companies as adversaries of the second sector: larger, established firms. The conventional portrayal envisions the nimble newcomers trying to outwit lumbering dinosaurs, who are in turn trying to flatten the upstarts. Something like that may occur at times, but a powerful symbiotic relationship is more common.

There are several ways in which new and established businesses work together. Most obvious, established firms often become customers of the new firms. U.S. corporations have learned to use new companies as reliable sources of innovation, buying from them, for example, specialized software and business services or components that can be embedded in their own products.

Large U.S. firms today effectively outsource much of their research and development to start-ups. Rather than take on all of the effort and risk of developing an idea internally, they help a new firm do so via strategic investments and working partnerships. There are many twists on this strategy. Intel, for example, tries to build markets for its chips by investing in companies that develop new systems and products that will use the chips; it has invested in more than a thousand such start-ups.

Once a new company develops a good product, a larger outfit often simply buys the start-up, thus acquiring a complete package of proven technology and expertise. This practice is now common in the pharmaceutical and health care product industries.

Mature firms support start-up firms by providing human capital. Bright young people often develop their skills and learn about a particular industry by working at a big corporation, then leave to start or join a new one.

The third important contributor to entrepreneurship is the government, which, in the United States, uses some of its tax revenues to foster new businesses. One way it does this is by funding large programs that traffic in innovation, such as defense and space exploration.

For example, the Department of Defense is always in the market for new systems and technologies, not only weaponry but also communications, intelligence, logistics, and support. Government agencies also invest directly in new firms through channels such as the Small Business Innovation Research program and the Central Intelligence Agency's In-Q-Tel venture fund. Total federal spending on research and development equals about one percent of U.S. GDP. Much of it flows into the fourth sector of the U.S. entrepreneurial system, the nation's universities.

U.S. universities generate a constant flow of ideas for new businesses. An invention or discovery moves out of a university into the entrepreneurial sector when investors and businesspeople help to form a company that commercializes the idea. It has been estimated that the companies spun out from just one university, the Massachusetts Institute of Technology, would constitute a nation with the twenty-fourth largest GDP in the world.

## We Have a Model

This four-sector model provides a useful framework for guiding policies to promote entrepreneurship in the developing world.

With respect to the first sector, developing nations must establish certain underlying conditions that allow the entrepreneurial process to flourish: favorable business policies and regulations, and access to investment and human capital.

U.S. laws make it easy to start, fund, grow, and sell a company. U.S. tax laws encourage private investment in new firms, and bankruptcy laws provide an orderly end to a failed business, reducing the risk for creditors and allowing entrepreneurs to start anew.

In many developing countries, by contrast, starting a business is fraught with expensive and time-consuming red tape. While all the paperwork for starting a corporation in the United States can be completed in a day, according to the World Bank it takes 153 days in Mozambique to incorporate and register a firm, 151 days in Indonesia, and 40 days in El Salvador. That must change. And more must be done overseas to promote a real symbiosis between established firms and entrepreneurs.

Developing countries must ensure that there is a level playing field between old and new firms. The United States tries to achieve this in a variety of ways, such as by protecting intellectual property and discouraging monopolies and unfair trade practices. Developing nations must resist pressures from existing businesses to preserve markets and prevent innovation.

The most promising entrepreneurs should be helped to find big corporations as partners, which in today's global economy can include corporations based in the United States or elsewhere. Developing countries' own large firms and government agencies also could be given incentives to support employees who have good ideas for starting spin-off companies.

In the government sector, nations should do as much as possible to invest in infrastructure that supports entrepreneurship. South Korea offers a good example with its efforts to promote end-user connectivity to the Internet. An estimated 60 to 70 percent of the country already has high-speed broadband access.

One rationale for this investment has been to make government more efficient and responsive by moving citizens' interactions online. But the policy is also helping to build a countrywide platform for entrepreneurship: every South Korean will soon be linked to massive online flows of knowledge and to online markets.

Another infrastructure investment beneficial to entrepreneurs is the subsidization of laboratories and testing facilities for shared use, which young technology firms often need but cannot afford on their own. Shared facilities also encourage entrepreneurs to cluster geographically, as they do in the United States—gathering in certain cities or around research universities—thereby gaining a dense network of peers for partnering and mentoring.

As to colleges and universities, the current approach rightly calls for countries to invest in education, but it emphasizes primary education. Higher education should be made a priority, too.

Consider India: in 1951, shortly after gaining independence, it launched the Indian Institute of Technology (IIT), modeling it on world-class universities such as MIT. This may be one of the best decisions a newly liberated nation ever made. IIT now has seven campuses across India. Its alumni make up part of India's formidable and growing professional class (the group from which many high-impact entrepreneurs emerge), and it has fueled interest in primary education by giving young Indians and their parents a great university toward which to aim.

Universities not only train skilled people but also attract them. In the United States, for example, about one-fourth of the new businesses in Silicon Valley since 1980 have been started by immigrants, many of whom were first drawn to the region to study or teach at its universities.

High-impact entrepreneurship will thrive most in countries that pay proper attention to all four sectors of the entrepreneurial system. China is an example of a developing nation that does. While adopting policies that actively encourage entrepreneurship, Beijing is pushing to have 20 percent more of its college-age population enrolled in higher education, for example. And it is developing high-skill, high-tech business in tandem with low-wage contract manufacturing, steelmaking, and other basic industries.

China seems to understand that the commodities it currently manufactures can be obtained from less developed countries and that many of the world's highly sought-after goods will come from laboratories, skilled people, and entrepreneurs. As a result, it may well arrive at its postindustrial stage very quickly.


## On Economics and Democracy

The classic formula for helping underdeveloped nations become part of the free world is to institute democracy first, then try to bring the economy up to speed. That has been the U.S. policy in Iraq, where the holding of elections was seen as pivotal. It has long been the policy of the European Union, which requires a candidate nation to have a fully functioning democracy before it can hope to reap the economic benefits of EU membership.

In the process of nation building, there are good reasons for trying to establish democracy early. But there is also evidence to suggest that the process may actually work better the other way around: that democracy—a system for political freedom—may take root best when it is preceded by, or at least accompanied by, economic freedom and a thriving economy.

Some of this evidence can be drawn from the Middle Ages in

continental Europe. While the feudal lords were able to maintain their rule in the agrarian countryside by savagely crushing peasant uprisings, the first successful stirrings toward personal liberty and self-governance came in the towns, which typically were centers of commerce and industry. Because of the value they created, the merchants and skilled craftsmen of the towns often gained freedom denied to others.

In time, because of the resources they controlled and the level of organization they came to have through their guilds, the merchants and craftsmen were able to assume political control. "Municipal democracy," wrote the historian Henri Pirenne, thus "set foot on the path which has been followed ever since."

The American Revolution also suggests the importance of a burgeoning economy as an antecedent to political reform. The movement that built the first national democracy was not triggered by an uprising of the masses; nor was it led by intellectual theorists. It was led by entrepreneurial men of means.

Paul Revere was a silversmith. Benjamin Franklin was an inventor and a businessman. Most signers of the Declaration of Independence were either merchants or professionals or, in the South, wealthy planters.

Not only did entrepreneurial capitalism pave the way to democracy, but the very process itself holds clues as to how the progression occurred and what the linkages were. Through business, many of the American founders gained the abilities needed to achieve and maintain self-governance.

In fact, starting a business develops precisely the traits that make democracy work. It requires independence, much effort, and self-discipline—but also the ability to work with others and the recognition that you can only succeed by serving the needs of others.

Franklin, the elder statesman of the movement, left copious

writings describing how he had honed his personal habits and diplomatic skills in the course of establishing himself as a printer. As for Revere, modern scholars have noted that he was a consummate networker who used his business contacts to help coordinate the revolutionary effort: when he set out on his Midnight Ride, he knew exactly where to go. Hamilton was a business prodigy who had managed a clerical office while still in his early teens; he later applied those skills to design the new nation's financial system.

Even Jefferson—Hamilton's adversary, who argued that the United States should remain a nation of farmers, and who held industry and commerce to be corrupting influences—was himself hardly the stereotypical rustic at the plow. He managed a sizable plantation. He eagerly sought new and more scientific ways to cultivate it. He designed buildings; he founded a university. In short, he was much more like the typical American entrepreneur: a striver and learner, often brimming with ego and unconventional opinions, but civic-minded and, in the end, a farsighted philanthropist.

Students studying the relationship of economics to democracy tend to portray the matter in terms of class. Conventional wisdom says, for instance, that the historic rise of democracy depended on the emergence of a bourgeoisie capable of contesting the aristocracy. Or similarly, that the maintenance of democracy depends on having a large and stable middle class. (Presumably, the trick lies in making this class numerous enough to discourage a power grab by insiders and prosperous enough that it won't fall prey to the rabble-rousing of demagogues.) But perhaps it is more accurate simply to say that the experience of economic freedom breeds both the skills and the inclination for political freedom.

## Why We Want to Go This Route

Encouraging entrepreneurship may do developing countries more good in terms of long-term growth and gains in productivity than policies aimed at accelerating near-term growth. As individuals step into the market, assume risk, and work to turn their aspirations into businesses, they will insist on political and economic liberalization—the very goals we seek.

Ironically, entrepreneurs, who are by nature agents of change, may prove to be among the most important forces for global stability since they promote freedom, which, after all, is at the heart of every nation that operates successfully for a long time. Freedom is more than being able to vote. It is the ability of individuals to live as they wish and pursue their desires. Democracy is a political system that protects personal freedom by giving people a hand in choosing their government, thereby making the government responsive to their wishes.

But the main way in which most people exercise freedom is through their work—through economic action. Viewed in that light, entrepreneurship may be the ultimate manifestation of individual freedom.

Merely by choosing occupations, people determine what kinds of activities they will engage in during most of their waking hours. In a healthy, diverse economy, there is a wide range of options. People can also choose how much their work means to them—it can be anything from just a way to earn a living to the central passion of life—and they can choose how to conduct their careers: seeking a niche, or seeking advancement, or shifting from one line of work to another.

The key to having all this freedom is abundance of opportunity. No economy, of course, can guarantee perfect outcomes. Not everyone can attain a dream job or earn an ideal income; every choice requires effort and entails risk. But a free economy *maximizes* opportunities. It offers many choices and many routes to the top. It offers the chance to change modes of work as personal needs or interests evolve, and to those who fail, it offers a chance to try again.

The overall result is that more value is created. Living standards are raised for all through increases in productivity and through putting new ideas and new technologies into play. In a sense, this merely repeats Adam Smith's famous observation that:

> By pursuing his own interest, [a man] frequently promotes that of the society more effectually than when he really intends to promote it. . . . The uniform, constant, and uninterrupted effort of every man to better his condition, the principle from which public and national, as well as private opulence is originally derived, is frequently powerful enough to maintain the natural progress of things toward improvement, in spite both of the extravagance of the government and of the greatest errors of administration.

But we now know that an invisible hand alone is not enough to drive a free-market economy. Long after Adam Smith, economists, notably Joseph Schumpeter, pointed out that it also requires innovation. Schumpeter wrote:

> The essential point to grasp is that in dealing with capitalism we are dealing with an evolutionary process. . . . Capitalism . . . is by nature a form or method of economic change and not only

never is but never can be stationary. . . . The fundamental impulse that sets and keeps the capitalist engine in motion comes from the new consumers' goods, the new methods of production or transportation, the new markets, the new forms of industrial organization that capitalist enterprise creates.

Recently, economist Paul Romer made the same point slightly differently:

We are not used to thinking of ideas as economic goods, but they are surely the most significant ones that we produce. . . . Economic growth occurs whenever people take resources and rearrange them in ways that are more valuable. . . . [It] springs from better recipes, not just from more cooking.

Such an economy is open to continual brainstorming and experimentation, which pays off because the people who make society—having a diverse mix of skills and different kinds of knowledge—are more likely to come up with and implement good ideas than any group of planners or experts. Thus, the very "un-plannedness" of a free economy, seemingly a great weakness, turns out to be a great strength.

Certainly a planned economy is capable of innovation. The Soviet Union stunned the world in the 1950s by being first into space. But the Soviet space program was the kind of thing state socialism does best: a massive command-and-control effort for a specific purpose. It generated little in the way of pervasive long-run economic benefits.

Meanwhile, Western capitalism was doing what it does best: calling forth innovation from all quarters and putting it to use for many purposes. In the United States during the postwar years, not only did the government pump increasing funds into research and development (including, belatedly, into a space program), but significant breakthroughs were made by scientists at private firms. And with widespread follow-on work by many, the fruits of innovation multiplied.

Consider just one chain of events. In 1947, a group at Bell Laboratories invented the transistor. In 1958, at the height of Sputnik mania, Jack Kilby at Texas Instruments expanded on the work at Bell Labs by inventing an integrated circuit, a silicon chip containing transistors along with other elements. Building off of these two innovations, others brought to market a series of new consumer and business goods, from transistor radios to pocket calculators and eventually personal computers—pioneered in the 1970s by entrepreneurs, at a time when existing firms did not yet see the value of PCs.

The PC industry, in turn, kick-started the fledgling software industry (which also had been launched by cadres of independent entrepreneurs). Advances in computing, in turn, enabled advances in biotechnology, a new field started by university researchers experimenting with recombinant DNA, which was then developed into an industry by entrepreneurs and venture capitalists.

No one could have planned these events. No one even foresaw them. Yet they led to entirely new industries employing millions and benefiting many millions more.

In the Soviet bloc—where progress was mapped out in five-year plans and where entrepreneurship was, to use computer terminology, not supported by the operating system—such industries never got off the ground. The Soviet system was capable of producing superbly trained scientists but literally incapable of capitalizing on their work.

By the 1980s, average per-capita incomes in the Soviet bloc

countries were well under half those in the United States, Western Europe, and Japan. The cost of this economic failure was twofold: most Soviet citizens could not afford to live as well as their Western counterparts; nor could many of them, even if employed, find meaningful and rewarding work.

Scientists and engineers were often unable to take part in applying the great discoveries of their time, as the relevant businesses had not grown there. Skilled mechanics and technicians were doomed to waste their talents in poorly run factories where production often bogged down because central planning had given them an oversupply of some materials but a shortage of others. People with white-collar talent had to toil in bureaucratic offices that were no better. And since there were no real mechanisms for entrepreneurial activity, people with ideas for new ventures or better ways of doing things could not act on their dreams. Many developing countries face the same institutional deficiencies today.

Ultimately, however, entrepreneurial capitalism is the most productive because it is the most dynamic form of economic activity. We should be doing everything in our power to encourage it worldwide.

There are clearly benefits for the United States in fostering a foreign policy based on the entrepreneurial imperative. If others copy our economy, we can expect that our own wealth will grow. A network of democracies practicing American entrepreneurial capitalism will become a virtual common market, more powerful than, say, the European Union.

Increased entrepreneurial activity worldwide increases our opportunities to sell goods and services to these rapidly emerging capitalist economies. We could also consolidate our roles as bankers and merchant bankers to the world.

In addition, the cluster of new democracies in Eastern Europe, if they settle on the U.S. model, will eventually force Old Europe to new growth and more democracy. (And in the process, of course, the power of France and Germany to thwart American foreign policy would be reduced.)

## Policy Implications

The policy of any developed nation should be focused on steering its own economy toward the entrepreneurial form of capitalism and on helping other nations move in that direction as well. These are places where both capitalism and democracy are still emerging or have only a tenuous hold. The twin systems must continue making progress together. Looking around the globe, we can find numerous regions that fit this description—Central and Eastern Europe immediately come to mind.

Many of the postcommunist nations in these places have been scoring impressive economic gains, and many claim to aspire to the American model. But most are not yet firmly on the way to entrepreneurial capitalism. For instance Slovakia, the self-styled "tiger of the Tatras," has had dramatic growth. But much of it thus far has come from foreign firms locating manufacturing and assembly plants there because of low labor costs and little corporate taxes. Unemployment still hovers above 15 percent, and not many significant new indigenous firms have started as yet.

Such countries must guard against overreliance on foreign investment—the trap often called dependent capitalism—and should use their low labor costs and tax rates as stepping stones, rather than counting on them as permanent advantages. The reason is obvious: others can match or underbid their rates.

One way the United States and others can help is by encouraging the growth of research universities in these countries. Many American universities are opening branches or finding affiliates overseas, a trend that should be encouraged. But a university alone is not enough. Countries must also build mechanisms to move university knowledge and talent out into the country's private sector, as occurs in many regions of the United States, from Silicon Valley to Austin and Boston.

For countries where democracy appears to be losing its grip, such as Russia, policy attention should be directed not so much at the country's political institutions but at its underlying economy. That is where problems often originate. Russia, for instance, relies heavily on exporting oil and minerals, which is dangerous on two counts. These income streams are susceptible to control by oligarchs and can lull a whole country into counting on easy money (as opposed to building value-added industry, which takes effort). Russia still has little idea-entrepreneurship for such a large country where so many are so highly educated.

The best way to help people around the world achieve political freedom is by maximizing their *economic* freedom. Of course, it is important to have stable democracies. But stability, ironically, is most likely to be found in nations capable of perpetually changing themselves. And that is not done just by voting. It is done by having entrepreneurial economies—the kind that invite all to experiment and innovate, the kind in which people can have a direct hand in creating their own futures every day.

We are and have been the most entrepreneurial economy on earth. It is the basis of our strength and wealth. Propagating our economic model will only make us and the rest of the world better off. Exporting entrepreneurial capitalism needs to be a core component of our foreign policy.

# 8

★

## IN CONCLUSION

*The new world of entrepreneurial capitalism*

THE ENTREPRENEURIAL IMPERATIVE IS CLEAR: **We either embrace a new and different view of our economic future, one that literally can make the world a better place, or we continue our current system that aims to satisfy the physical needs of a relatively tiny portion of the globe.**

The prevailing world model—bureaucratic capitalism—aggregates capital in the hands of a relatively small number of people and countries. This inevitably leads to conflict. At the very least, those who don't have that capital are envious and hostile. At the very worst, they will plot and scheme to take that capital away from those who have it—by all means necessary.

But the implicit reasoning behind this model is wrong. It assumes the worldwide economic pie is limited. If I get a bigger slice, you must get a smaller one. That simply is not the case.

Implicit in the entrepreneurial imperative is that the economic pie can get bigger. That is the first promise of the entrepreneurial economy. The second is it brings a much deeper human dimension

to economic activity. It says that individuals can control their economic destiny by expressing their creativity and urge to help others
through the medium of moving ideas into the market by forming
new entrepreneurial firms. Third, because entrepreneurial capitalism requires individuals to act on their own behalf, it holds the
promise of changing deeply entrenched cultural assumptions about
business.

In the old economic model, in which capital was limited to the
hands of a few, business was a mysterious process that only people
with money understood. In the entrepreneurial economy, the
processes of business become clear because, by definition, more
people participate in the process. When people see working for
themselves in the private sector as a possibility, then business serves
as a force in the democratization of the political world.

## The New World Order

As we have seen, a wholesale introduction of the entrepreneurial
imperative will lead to the world economy growing everywhere. It
is not dependent on natural resources or the accumulation of
wealth over time but on the initiative and applied intelligence of
individuals.

As Americans, not only do we want to embrace this concept,
we want to make it the basis of our foreign policy. Exporting American entrepreneurial economics holds the potential to do more for
expanding American markets, securing our position in world banking, and strengthening our university system than any other thing
we might do. It also holds the potential to do more for the expansion and distribution of wealth than any step other nations might
take, leading to worldwide political stability.

Marxism envisioned a rather static store of capital distributed through an ideological, not practical, system that proved unacceptable to those who lived under it. Capitalism has been secure because of its presumed and proven ability to achieve expansion of wealth. But in both systems the distribution of wealth was and is a continuing political problem. In communism, despite the rhetoric of "from each according to his ability to each according to his needs," wealth always ends up in the hands of a few. Capitalism faces a chronic but not insignificant problem of ensuring widespread participation in the creation of wealth.

Entrepreneurial capitalism holds the potential of solving the distribution conundrum. As individual initiative and intellectual talent increasingly become the motors of wealth creation, the ability to make wealth and to expand social welfare grows.

Entrepreneurial capitalism holds the hope of protecting capitalism and its most important dependency, namely, democracy itself. That is why I have referred throughout to the concept as the entrepreneurial imperative. We have no other choice but to exploit this concept to the fullest if we wish America to remain a superpower.

The idea that our future depends on entrepreneurs and the entrepreneurial ecosystem is all the more surprising when we think back on the perspective that prevailed in the minds of the world's greatest economists just a few years ago. They had concluded that the future of the economy was settled: big business, big labor, and big unions would work together to produce steady and predictable growth. Wealth distribution would occur through the steady expansion of employment in corporate conglomerates, employer-provided benefits, and government transfer payments.

These views become widespread for a reason. They were advocating exactly what the people running big business, big government, and big labor wanted to hear.

Government officials saw themselves saving capitalism through activist policies, so they committed to what they read in Keynes, Galbraith, and Drucker. These men had provided government bureaucrats with well-reasoned academic arguments as to why creating programs that made citizens dependent on federal spending was the proper path to the future.

And business leaders could hardly be expected to resist being hailed as the true heroes of capitalism by business school professors, who had studied these economists and concluded that entrepreneurial activity was messy, unpredictable, and the province of "propeller heads"—the quirky inventors. And union leaders, too, were thrilled by the conclusions of economic experts who assumed the role of unions was preordained.

Still, surely by the time (1993) Drucker expressed his view that we would never see the likes of Rockefeller and Ford again, someone should have seen that companies such as Microsoft, Oracle, Intel, Compaq, and Hewlett Packard—all of which were being written about in the business press at the time—were not the invention of large business bureaucracies but rather the creation of entrepreneurs who were present-day look-alikes of the people who created Standard Oil, U.S. Steel, and AT&T a century before. The point, however, is that the entrepreneurial imperative is all the stronger because of the unexpected emergence of great entrepreneurs who changed the course of history with the communications and information processing revolutions. And, of course, we have seen how their innovations are democratizing business—anyone can start a company!—and how entrepreneurial capitalism is spreading democracy itself by serving as a model of what the new world economy could be.

## Adjusting to This Brave New World

So what does this all mean for us and our children going forward? The answer to that, too, is counterintuitive. The history of the last twenty years confirms a disquieting conundrum that is the subtext of this book: the *less* secure we are economically, the *more* secure we are economically. The more new (good) ideas and new (innovative) companies surface to replace the old, the stronger our economy is.

To participate in this brave new world, we need to start here: Students must get a great education, not merely a great degree. We are in a period when universities will gladly declare anyone educated in exchange for receiving tuition checks for four years. That is not particularly helpful. All those who aspire to success must take charge of their education and make sure they are learning things and acquiring skills that might ready them for the future.

The second thing that needs to be done involves mentoring. Studies show that the rate of success of a new business start-up can be improved by a factor of at least three if the entrepreneur has a mentor. Good mentors have been through the process of starting a business and can offer dispassionate and objective advice at certain steps along the way. All entrepreneurs can benefit from mentors.

But identifying someone who will be truly helpful as a mentor is a difficult task. Most people are pleased to talk. Successful people are generally very happy to recall how they "made it." But that is not the same thing as providing useful and valuable advice.

The best mentors are people who failed once or twice and had many difficulties in the birthing of their companies. People don't generally advertise their travail, so it may take some digging and some acute interviewing to find the right mentor. A good mentor is dispassionate—he or she will not want and should not have an equity stake in your business. Advice should be given freely.

Step three? Stick to it. Successful businesses seldom happen overnight. And they are almost never identical to what is envisioned on the day the business begins. Sometimes people catch the wrong wave and invest in a technology that becomes obsolete overnight— a competitor appears with a better mousetrap. Bad luck, that's all.

The process of becoming an entrepreneur is an ongoing learning experience. If one business fails, it becomes a perfect case study in what decisions were wrong. Learn from those mistakes. Success teaches little. Failure is the best school for entrepreneurs. It is from this struggle that real entrepreneurs emerge. In fact, serial entrepreneurs, who go from one successful company to another, almost uniformly point to the failures and struggles in their first business as the secret to their subsequent success.

The fourth thing: As soon as possible, entrepreneurs should do something to nurture the system that allowed them to emerge. Obviously, they must give of their time as mentors, working with students either directly or by starting and supporting college-level programs that encourage entrepreneurship. In the future, it is imperative that every institution of higher education understand the importance of entrepreneurial activity for the nation's future and prepare its students for the new economy.

Learning entrepreneurship does not begin by teaching accounting, finance, and business plan writing. Much more important is learning how to apply creativity in math or chemistry or biology to a business idea. Opportunity recognition—recognizing a need in the marketplace—is the central focus. Introducing a product or service that fills a need is the best way for the innovator to impact the greatest number of lives.

But, more than this, successful entrepreneurs must give back in other ways. One of the most important is to make angel capital available to other entrepreneurs. As many entrepreneurs know, the struggle to get capital resources is not easy. Venture capital funds have become much more removed from the process of starting up promising companies. They are now, as we have noted, largely sources of mezzanine financing, providing the last round of funding before a company goes public or is sold. Many firms need capital, and angels can not only provide money but also can accompany it with sound advice.

## Going Forward

For the United States to continue its global leadership, it must help the world see clearly the breadth and depth of our economic evolution. Our entrepreneurial economy is all about the freedom of creative and highly educated people to fulfill all of their potential.

Our economic clockworks operate to support entrepreneurs. We encourage their risk taking by preparing them for self-employment. Our strong economy protects them from failure by providing employment with others if their venture does not succeed. We make sufficient investment capital available to them through:

- Angel investors
- A supply of ample venture capital for companies that have high growth potential
- Easily accessed public equity markets

All this adds up to the complicated miracle of the American entrepreneurial economy. Our public policy must be focused on making the system stronger and more efficient. Preparing college students for entrepreneurial careers is one such action. Making sure our tax policy is simple and stimulates investment in start-up firms is another. Double-checking to see that potential laws won't gum up the economic works is a third.

It is in Americans' interest to see our system replicated all over the world. We must believe that in flourishing entrepreneurial economies the widening distribution of wealth and the creation of new jobs will naturally help lead to the spread of democracy.

Entrepreneurship cannot work well under any other system. People who have built businesses want to protect their wealth and will insist on predictable systems of government that are first and foremost participatory.

Entrepreneurial capitalism is a departure from all previous systems. While built on our history, it is a step in the direction of millions of people controlling businesses that support an unprecedented explosion of human creativity and the expansion of human security and wealth.

It is imperative that we—everyone everywhere—go into this entrepreneurial future together.

★ *It is easy to imagine entrepreneurial capitalism being part of the campaign platform that helps elect the next president of the United States. If the president were to ask me for advice following his or her inauguration, here is what I'd say.* ★

*Dear Mr. or Ms. President of the United States,*
Congratulations upon achieving the most important job in the world. Your vision of the future—where we all will be members of the Entrepreneurial

Society—clearly resonated with the voters. And now you have the opportunity to influence the welfare of the nation and the world for generations to come.

Implementing your vision will lead to unparalleled levels of domestic prosperity and prove to be the soundest basis for international economic growth. When in place, it can achieve the most elusive of goals: a domestic policy that serves as an easily understood foundation for our foreign relations, one that reflects the noblest aspirations of this country for expanding liberty for all the citizens of the world.

That, of course, will lead to expanding world security. As you said throughout the campaign, very few people who are doing well economically want to risk that financial security by going to war. You were prescient when you said, "Making the Entrepreneurial Society work is America's next and perhaps last chance to show the world the promise of self-government and what freedom means to the future of the world."

Because your margin of victory was so wide, you will truly have a chance to implement the new economic theory that you described during the campaign. As so often happens in politics, your campaign benefited by having caught the wave of what has been happening for a long while—three decades in our case—but has been almost invisible to the average voter and certainly to the political elite. Voters already had a sense of what you were saying about the change in the economy. They have come to see entrepreneurs in a very positive light and had an intuition that new, highly entrepreneurial companies like Google, eBay, Amazon, and many others are vital to the nation's evolving economy. Indeed, with these types of firms creating more than half the new jobs in the United States, the image you painted of the entrepreneurial economy really helped voters see what they had already sensed.

More and more people hope to see their children graduate from college and start a business, to take risk, and swing for the fences. Gone are the days, thank goodness, when parents aspired to government jobs for their kids.

Your message to younger voters that they can work for themselves, that they can create their own jobs, and control their own economic destiny, held great appeal. One reason is that many younger voters know people who have already gone down this path. There is a broad intuition in the country that starting a business is becoming more common and less risky.

Your message to minorities and immigrants was especially important in winning the election, but that shouldn't have been surprising. More than any other segment of the population, minorities have higher aspirations for starting and owning their own businesses. Your message that you could see an America where the ranks of millionaires and billionaires had many blacks and Hispanics, as well as women, tapped into their dreams of real commercial success. No wonder these voters said your promise of creating an "equal opportunity to achieve" resonated.

In fact, it is time to create a serious program directed toward minorities that will help them prepare for the tough world of business ownership. This would not be a new program from the Small Business Administration. There is no reason to talk "small" when we discuss minority-owned businesses. The nation must help identify, recruit, coach, and support minority businesspeople who have technology skills and the ability to build sizable new businesses. To help a sizable cadre of highly successful minority business owners to develop would be to push against the last frontiers where minorities have not achieved in ways comparable to the majority population. (This is not the job of the SBA.) If you can make this happen, you will be writing the next chapter in the resolution of the legacy of racial discrimination.

Your vision is equal to the Great Society, and just as President

Johnson's vision was right for the time, so is yours for today. Just as Johnson saw the Great Society as changing the culture of America, you see that long-term success requires each of us to become an active participant in the Entrepreneurial Society.

Going forward, management of the macroeconomic environment is of the greatest importance. No one can be allowed to forget what we had to deal with before the entrepreneurial economy came to the fore. Inflation proved to be the worst scourge of modern times, robbing people of their savings and making wages less and less valuable. Not only was this demoralizing in itself, it was accompanied by an erosion of American purchasing power in world markets and a degradation in America's role in world affairs.

The lessons from the painful and dangerous period when bureaucratic capitalism fell apart should never be forgotten. A strong central banking system, clear policy from the Treasury, and intelligent action in Congress in making fiscal policy are all important to ensure that the economy continues to focus on growth above all.

You must convince Congress to keep taxes low to help ensure a congenial environment for new business creation. Without new businesses and economic growth, there can be no improvement in the welfare of all citizens.

Also, the tax code needs to change. Earnings on savings should be exempt from taxation up to 5 percent of income so that individuals have a strong incentive to save. And taxes on business investments that produce a strong return should be relatively low so that there are also strong incentives to encourage everyone to participate in the entrepreneurial economy. For people who put a portion of their savings or investments into start-up firms as angels—directly investing in the new company or as members of a venture capital partnership—there should be even more favorable capital gains treatment so that this type of investing becomes widespread.

In addition, since you have the rarest of gifts—the ability to make a speech to millions that actually teaches—you must explain to the nation that government action does not create wealth. That's why you need to cut spending on benefit programs and reduce the overhead of the federal government, in part by reshaping legislation that bears on business, especially new businesses.

As the nation's tutor, you must make it plain that we cannot regulate ourselves into a nation of wealth. Only individual citizens working in the private sector can make wealth, which in turn can be shared with others. You must make it clear to everyone that the creation and growth of private companies is the only way wealth is made. Ensuring that the greatest number of people are engaged in making new companies successful should be the central focus of policy.

What other steps should you take to make the Entrepreneurial Society a successful and sustaining part of America's future?

Obviously, educational reform is at the top of everyone's agenda. You have an opportunity to focus your policy on the improvement of science, technology, engineering, and mathematics (STEM) and set the teaching of these subjects in the context of entrepreneurial business.

By making science/math and entrepreneurship the new focus for every high school in the United States—by stressing that the nation needs many more scientists, mathematicians, and engineers ready to start or work in new high-tech businesses—suddenly the conversation changes. If we start with the premise that we need more people trained in STEM, what naturally follows is we need more people to teach those subjects. And that leads to the conclusion that we need a completely new stream of teachers to staff a new vision of what our high schools should look like.

Our nation's teaching colleges cannot provide the teachers we need. We don't need more education majors who know a little about science and math. We need math and science majors who know about how entrepreneurial businesses work and who can teach.

Change cannot stop at high school. Our nation's universities need attention, too. We need the universities to ready the next generation for the radically changing roles that successive generations must play to keep America thriving and to sustain American values of freedom and liberty. Not only should they teach entrepreneurship—not as a separate but as an integrated part of the business, history, and social sciences curriculum—but our colleges should model the behavior themselves. The American university should be the most entrepreneurial of our institutions. As you know, they are not. Unfortunately, many are becoming hopelessly bureaucratic.

There is a growing body of evidence that suggests university research productivity is falling. Because the basic research performed in universities is more and more important to our future, it is critical that you create incentives for universities to improve their productivity.

One way to stimulate a renaissance of university research is to propose a massive new federal research objective. Solving the problem of fossil fuel dependency is just the type of problem that our universities would respond to with excellence. This is the single biggest chronic problem that faces the nation's economy and the world's environment. Our nation's great research universities would be rejuvenated by the challenge just as they were by the nation's commitment to space research and by the challenge of curing cancer.

While it is hard for the federal government to get involved in specific curriculum matters, it is worth creating a dialogue about what business schools might do to help the emerging economy. If ever there was part of the university trapped in the old economy, it is the nation's business schools. They just don't seem to get the importance of entrepreneurial activity. As president, you should make a point of speaking at a few business schools and take the message that the country needs more people trained at helping entrepreneurs.

## WHERE BIG COMPANIES AND THE GOVERNMENT FIT IN

Most successful big businesses have navigated the transformation in the economy and have become more entrepreneurial themselves. When big companies rediscover their entrepreneurial past, great things happen. They grow faster; divest unproductive assets, frequently selling them to more entrepreneurial people or companies that know what to do with them; and become more responsive to their customers.

That's great. But we need to do more. As a nation, we should seek to have, say, a million new business start-ups every year (nearly twice present levels). Entrepreneurs should be encouraged with readily available government research dollars for seed projects; thus, the flow of dollars to entrepreneurs through the various federal departments should be expanding at, say, 5 percent every year for a decade.

Now it is time to build a culture that embraces insecurity and disruption, viewing them as central to helping people achieve their greatest creative ability and, if appropriate, to work out their futures and their careers in highly innovative firms. To achieve this, the federal bureaucracy must conceive of its purpose in different terms. It must be refocused on helping Americans everywhere. With the extraordinary change underway in all parts of America, it is probably time to decentralize the federal government.

By moving most of the federal departments away from Washington, the bureaucracy will become more sensitive and responsive to the needs of the new economy and the entrepreneurial aspirations of our citizens. By relocating departments, the government can reshape its internal cultures. Think of the Department of Transportation headquartered in Colorado and the Department of Health and Human Services in Seattle. Many agencies could be spread around the country. In an age of frictionless communication and a concern that the entire government should not be massed together for security's sake, the geographic distribution of federal functions makes strategic sense as well as cultural sense.

Our national ecosystem must also be strengthened by solving the problems of financing corporate pensions and benefits and the public obligations of Social Security and Medicare. If there is one overarching lesson in political economy that the postwar generation of business, union, and government leaders should have taught us, it is never believe that the future will look like the present. Union contracts that secured benefits in the 1960s turned out to be part of the clockworks, along with the failure of management to innovate, which unwound the auto companies themselves. Government's promises to pay for health care and to ensure that Social Security was indexed for inflation turned out to be part of the economic burden that is slowing down our economy. It seems that when we promise ourselves future benefits through the instrument of government or business or unions, we influence history in a bad way.

In trying to fix these problems, and prevent their coming back, the appropriate wisdom is that individuals must guard their own future security through the management of their health spending and their pensions. There is overwhelming evidence that private pension management has turned out to be good for the individual and good for the economy, including making it more entrepreneurial.

Markets respond to demand, and every step should be taken to em-

184

power individuals to spend money that is either their own or (for the poor) comes in the form of vouchers from government to buy their own health care and save for their future.

America is a nation of immigrants. We must realize that for the nation to continue to grow, we will need more and more immigrants to come to America, to learn how to speak English as our forebears did, to study and get well educated, and to assume productive roles as citizens. Many of our smartest people are Americans who were born abroad, who came to study advanced technology, and who embraced America as the land of opportunity. We must keep this wonderful part of our history healthy and working. To achieve high levels of immigration of the best and brightest from around the world, we should grant citizenship to any foreign student graduating from a four-year university who declares his or her intent to embrace all the best of American life.

## BUILDING AN ECONOMIC ECOSYSTEM

As you have seen, your agenda cannot be just a laundry list of new programs. Making the Entrepreneurial Society work requires that old views of government's role in the economy and in society must be undone. You must bring forth a comprehensive vision of the Entrepreneurial Society. If you don't do this, you can be sure that many people working in Washington and elsewhere will choose not to "get it" and will wait you out, ready to reinvigorate their bureaucratic visions of how America is supposed to work, using federal regulations to implement their ideal once you leave office.

In the recent past, presidents have come to the White House with either modest visions of what their economic agenda should be or visions that were incomplete. Our nation cannot go into the future with unimaginative, piecemeal, and thin visions of economic policy. We need a robust vision of where the economy is headed and public policy that will ensure the likelihood that the new economy will emerge.

Getting the policy right is more important than ever before, because with each passing year it is clear that the economic policy apparatus in the United States and our economic institutions are central to how other countries govern their economies. The Federal Reserve is the world's central bank. The stock exchanges of New York must remain the world's preeminent capital markets. And the decisions we make—everything from free trade to the cost of government social benefits—here in the United States have implications for growth rates around the world.

Without a clearly articulated alternative, we will continue to watch the world do dangerous things. The growing bureaucracy of Europe will continue to choke its member countries' economies. Europe seems to think that the EU can legislate a dynamic economy even in the face of high unemployment and low levels of economic growth.

The inability of European economies to keep up may lead to a dangerous challenge to capitalism. In the minds of many in Old Europe, and with the apparent inability of many of the Eastern European economies to grow, the socialist path may not look so bad. Sadly, the American alternative—the proven position that free markets will produce more wealth for everyone—is not a view that is universally seen for its absolute truth.

Our partisan combat in Congress has done much to cloud our own vision on this topic where we operate to protect certain American market positions with tariffs and trade barriers. The continued rant regarding the loss of jobs overseas, however, is a thinly veiled strategy to protect lower paid manufacturing jobs in the United States.

Our hands are not clean because our thinking is not clear. Politics is messy, but we can't send a message to the world that free markets are good for everyone else but not for us.

The Entrepreneurial Society envisions that all Americans have an entrepreneurial role to play, that they understand the process and the importance of innovation and personal creativity and the legitimacy of business as an outlet for human potential. America has always been a land where every individual can pursue a particular route to success and contribute to the general welfare of his or her community and the nation.

When every American is working at his or her own entrepreneurial contribution, the nation will be well poised to hold its own against Chinese, Indian, and all other foreign competition. Moreover, we will be modeling for the world how a society can work for everyone's benefit.

Good luck.

# INDEX

★